Work and the Evolving Self

Theoretical and Clinical Considerations

Work and the Evolving Self

Theoretical and Clinical Considerations

Steven D. Axelrod

THE ANALYTIC PRESS

1999   Hillsdale, NJ   London

Published by
The Analytic Press, Inc.
Editorial offices:
101 West Street
Hillsdale, New Jersey 07642
www.analyticpress.com

Typeset in Adobe Caslon by CompuDesign, Rego Park, NY

Library of Congress Cataloging-in-Publication Data

Axelrod, Steven D., 1951–   .
    Work and the evolving self : theoretical and clinical considerations /
Steven D. Axelrod.
        p.   cm.
    Includes bibliographical references and index.
    ISBN 0-88163-207-4
    1. Industrial psychiatry.   2. Work—Psychological aspects.
3. Quality of work life.   I. Title.
RC967.5.A95 1999
616.89'14—dc21   98-48420
                                                                      CIP

Printed in the United States of America
10   9   8   7   6   5   4   3   2   1

To my father and mother,
who showed me the value of work.

Acknowledgments

Writing is solitary, often lonely work. The quiet it requires, though, is filled with a multitude of inner voices—authors we've admired, teachers, analysts, parents, friends, lovers, patients. And somewhere out of that mix, our ideas and experiences coalesce on the page.

I am fortunate to have had Fred Pine and Sheldon Bach as my teachers, and they have contributed greatly to my intellectual development. Pine's articulation of a clinically based multimodel approach to psychoanalysis informs all my work; I feel deeply identified with it. Bach's ideas on the self and narcissism changed the way I understand and work with patients and helped kindle my interest in work and the ego ideal.

Martin Bergmann has been a model to me of the psychoanalyst/author. His love of psychoanalysis, openness to new ideas, and intellectual vigor have been inspirational. I am sorry that Donald Kaplan didn't live to read this book and debate some of its ideas with me; his encouragement early on meant a lot to me. Charles Spezzano, who discusssed my first paper on work, was also encouraging at a critical juncture. Harry Levinson, a trailblazer in applying psychoanalytic thinking to management, took the time to read some of my early papers on work and offered valuable suggestions. My colleague, good friend, and intellectual double, Michael Diamond, has also been an important source of support as well as a model of authorial energy.

If it is generally true that our patients teach us most of what we know, that is especially the case with this project. This book grew directly out of my clinical work and my attempts to incorporate work issues into my practice. I owe an enormous debt of gratitude to my patients, and I hope that with this book I can begin to repay it.

As this project developed beyond its formative stages, actual links to the world of work became increasingly important. I want to thank Fred Doolittle of the Manpower Research Demonstration Project. Larry Hirschhorn of The Center for Applied Research, Dennis O'Neill of NY Life, Larry Erlbaum of Lawrence Erlbaum Associates, and Toby Herr of Project Match for their time in discussing with me their perspectives on changes in the workplace. Members of the Work and Psychoanalysis Study Group gave me encouragement and useful feedback on some of the material in the book. Special thanks are due to Steve Lurie and Bruce Hammer of Lutie Executive Development for giving me a chance to apply my ideas to executive coaching and being there for me when it really mattered.

My sons, Ben and Nick, understood how important this project was to me, and I appreciate the many allowances they made. Thanks to Sandy for encouraging me to get it done. And, finally, I want to thank my friends at The Analytic Press. Paul Stepansky believed in this book from the beginning. He was patient with me as a first-time author and engaged me in a challenging and fruitful dialogue about what to include in the book and how to develop my ideas. Thanks also to John Kerr for his thoughtful reading of the manuscript and to Eleanor Starke Kobrin (Lenni) for her expert copy editing and good humor.

Contents

Preface

Why does an author write a particular book? What are the sources of his interest in the topic? How have the author's conflicts and defensive style determined both the content and the form of the work? Who is the author's inner audience, and how is he trying to influence them? And how is the author trying to transform himself by writing the book? Would he have written it differently at a different time in his life?

Chances are that the author is in a better position to answer these questions, to plumb the depths of his involvement in the project, when he has completed it. Then he may come to realize that the book he would write if he were to start over would probably be very different from the one that is "finished." It can be a sobering experience for the author to realize that the ways in which he would work out the central problems of the book will continue to change over time as he continues to grow and develop.

This is a book on work. In it, I describe how I think about and approach patients' work lives in the clinical setting. My interest is in showing how our analytic skills and intimate knowledge of our patients' inner lives can most effectively be used to strengthen their work functioning and to enhance their lives and promote growth. Even today, the choice of topic is an unusual one for a psychoanalyst—there is little in the way of books and articles in the psychoanalytic literature and very few professional lectures or conferences devoted to the topic. So why my interest in the topic? What does it say about me personally and as a psychoanalyst? Perhaps my choice of topic can teach my colleagues something about our professional identities as psychoanalysts in an era that seems particularly stressful for all of us.

Most men of my generation came to know our fathers largely through what they did for a living. It was the 1950s, and the "work ethic" seemed to be seamlessly woven into the fabric of our culture. Elsewhere (Axelrod, 1997) I have written about the son's essential difficulty knowing his father. It has historically been largely through what the boy sees the father do, how the father works, and how he acts on the world that the son apprehends the father. An understanding of the father's place in the world, what he does and how he does it, gives the child a real sense of the father. It is sometimes this sense of the father that endures, while more confusing and conflictual feelings are repressed.

The interest in fathering that has blossomed over the last 20 years (Cath, Gurwitt, and Ross, 1982; Cath, Gurwitt, and Gunsberg, 1989; Ross, 1994; Shapiro, Diamond, and Greenberg, 1995) has revolved around the nurturing father, the father who is an active participant in the intimate sphere of the family. Of course, this interest has been driven by economic and workforce changes that have made women less available for traditional parenting. The hope has been that the father will become less absent and more real to the children who need him. And, although many of us strive to be better fathers in this sense, I believe that to some extent we will continue to be mysterious figures to our children, known, perhaps more than we would like, by how we act in the world outside the family.

While my parents personified the cultural values of their era, I believe they went a step further than many in their emphasis on work. Both my father and my mother were hard working and more comfortable working than playing. Real enjoyment was derived from earning a living, building a business, and managing a home and family. Achievement was probably *the* dominant value. One gained recognition largely by work and accomplishment. Work was at the core of family life.

This scene may sound dour and boring by today's standards, and in some ways it was. Yet there was pride and excitement in my parents' work lives, and my connection to them included sharing these emotions. My father had built his own business and was exceptionally proud of his accomplishment. He was respected and admired by his extended family for his businessman's savvy. When from early childhood I walked the factory floor with my father, I acquired a sense of his importance and felt important too. I was fussed over by secretaries and greeted by clerks and machine operators. I was interested in how things worked and how people did their jobs. I repaid their attention with curiosity.

Later I became interested not only in how things worked and how people did their jobs, but in the conditions of those jobs. It was the 60s, unions were still important, and I was perplexed and angry about why my father fought unionization of his factory. It was the time of the Vietnam War, and antiunion and prowar sentiments became conflated in my mind. If my father the engineer specialized in production, I would specialize in the people processes that he seemed inadequately attuned to both at home and at work. I spent one summer during this turbulent period assisting the company's personnel director, someone my father seemed to view with a mix of curiosity (as if from a different species), suspicion, and grudging respect. My interest in personnel (now called human resources), the human side of businees, preceded and helped give rise to my interest in psychology. Thus, although like that of many psychologists, my career choice reflected my wishes to heal myself and my family of origin, it had another important determinant. I would stake out my own territory and win an important father son battle by devoting my work life to people problems and their resolution.

In graduate school in the 1970s the intensity of clinical training left little room for me to pursue an interest in workplace issues. Becoming a therapist (and later an analyst) is a very absorbing experience that leaves little room for what may be considered peripheral interests. A few of us spent a semester exploring the integration of Freudian and Marxist concepts and came up empty handed. Erikson's writings on work and identity didn't seem to speak much to the alienating and dehumanizing nature of most jobs. Fromm seemed more sociologist than depth psychologist. *Work and career issues were not part of the curriculum in graduate school, nor would they be in my psychoanalytic training.* Instead, work and career seemed to be the domain of counseling psychologists, and, although I knew next to nothing of what they actually did, I "knew" counseling couldn't hold a candle to the romance of psychoanalysis. The only literature on the work place I found compelling was that on hospital milieus, the contribution of patient-staff dynamics to patient symptomatology and recovery. This was the beginning of my interest in organizational dynamics and led to the writing of my first paper, "Staff Interaction and Therapeutic Structure on a Short-Term Psychiatric Unit" (Axelrod and Axelrod, 1987).

After completing graduate school, I continued to work in hospitals. But already career opportunities for psychologists were beginning to change, foreshadowing the upheaval brought on by managed care in the 1990s. Opportunities began to diminish for psychologists to take on teaching and supervising roles in hospitals on the basis of their clinical psychoanalytic skills. Technical skills (neuropsychological, research, specialty populations) became increasingly important as biological psychiatry gained ascendance. I started to rethink my focus on hospital work and began psychoanalytic training, aiming to build a full-time practice supplemented by institute-based teaching. By the late 80s, however, there was no denying that psychoanalytic patients were becoming rare and that private practice was changing. It was the Reagan era, and as our culture wholeheartedly embraced the entrepreneurial ethos we began to hear that, as practitioners, we too would have to adopt, in some way, business practices—partnerships, marketing, specialization, diversification of "products." Like many executives and professionals who come face to face with downsizing, I found it extremely difficult to accept the changes I would have to make in my expectations and in my very approach to my career.

These changes in my own workplace acted in synergy with my second analysis to challenge my defenses. I had to confront the ways in which my own ego ideal served passive and avoidant trends in my personality. Implicitly, I had thought private practice would be a haven from the heartless, profit-driven world of business—from the world, that is, of my father. In this respect I was, unconsciously, using my career as a means to avoid confronting my own Oedipus complex. Economic and cultural changes, on one hand, and my own analysis, on the other, conspired against this neurotic solution. If times had been different, I *might* have been able to avoid dealing with these issues in relation to my work life. As it was, the inhibitions that affected my work life became a major focus of my treatment. I came to see that to be effective I would have to blend my own reflectiveness with an interest in the world of action, not inhibit it out of deference and fear.

As I began to wrestle with my own work inhibition and to synthesize the different strands of my identity as a psychoanalyst, I became interested in my patients' work lives—not just how they related to others in the workplace, but how they related to work itself. How did their difficulties working in a vital and productive fashion express core conflicts and developmental themes? As I listened, I found the material compelling but discovered that little had been written in the psychoanalytic literature about work. I was on my way to writing the first of a series of papers on work and the ego ideal.

At first, I was careful not to venture too far from the consulting room and the traditional framework of individual, psychoanalytic treatment. I was interested in actual workplace applications of what I was starting to explore and write about, but I was wary. I wanted to maintain my identity as a psychoanalyst, first and foremost, and to uphold my version of the analytic ideal.

Pushed by market forces, my own interest in the workplace, and a personal analysis that helped me relinquish some of my own rigid categorizations and counteridentifications, my interests evolved further. Good fortune intervened, and I linked up with a management consulting firm doing executive assessment and coaching. I also began to learn about vocational assessment and career counseling from a clinician's perspective. These changes were both exciting and frightening. I found that I liked the activity and stimulation of "being out in the world." Yet, what about my identity as an analyst?

Although I never intended it this way, this book in many ways charts the course of my own evolution as a psychoanalyst interested in work-related issues. Following initial chapters that are more metapsychological and developmental in the traditional psychoanalytic sense, I turn to "work disturbance" and its treatment in clinical practice. By the time I get to the chapter on "Vocational Development in Individual Treatment," the distinctions among counseling, therapy, and analysis have begun to blur. If I had included a chapter on executive coaching in an organizational setting, even more questions could have been raised—what about confidentiality, about the client's responsibility for payment? The final chapter, on "The Changing Workplace," owes a heavier debt to management theory than to psychoanalytic thinking.

Like other clinicians striving to adapt to a changing workplace, I have had to think long and hard about my identity as a psychoanalyst. And the reader of this book may well ask what the relationship is between some of the work-related interventions I am advocating and the rest of the patient's psychoanalytically oriented treatment. How does one square some of the more directive approaches (especially those in Chapter 8) with a psychoanalytically oriented treatment? I encourage the reader to use this as an orienting question to the book both because it may enhance an understanding of the issues I present and because it will help refine one's own sense of oneself as an analyst during a challenging and difficult era.

Let me add a note on the issue of psychoanalytic purity. Wallerstein (1986), in his important book on the Menninger Psychotherapy Research Project, challenged the ideal of analytic purity. Truly effective analytic treatment, he found, included the more active interventions that were typically thought of as therapy, even counseling. I strongly believe that those of us who are more wedded to effectiveness than to purity must rethink the value of the analyst's activity and be sensitized to the perils of the analyst's defensive passivity.

Wallerstein suggested that interventions that are more active and directive, even if not analytic per se, can be consistent with an analytic treatment. Perhaps we should be more open to thinking of treatment as movement back and forth between more directive interventions focusing on external reality and more exploratory, intrapsychically focused interventions. A key issue here, I believe, is to keep the patient's goals clearly in mind. Patients have goals on many different levels, from relief of symptoms, to more effective adaptation in different life spheres, to increased comfort with inner experience. I believe we should take these goals seriously and do what we can to help our patients achieve them. Doing so certainly does not preclude our inclination as analysts not to take our patients' goals just at face value but to subject them to ongoing scrutiny.

When I consult on a vocational counseling or executive coaching case, I view the case differently because of my analytic understanding and experience. What exactly does this mean? I believe that psychic determinism, principles of unconscious motivation, and core psychodynamic themes (separation-individuation, Oedipus complex, identity formation, typical sources of anxiety, the critical roles of shame, guilt, and other affects, and so forth) are powerful tools of understanding *regardless of the context of the intervention.* An understanding of the roles of transference, countertransference, and resistance can inform the clinician's understanding of the client, whatever mode of treatment is practiced.

As an analyst, I try to consider the context of my interventions in terms of its goals and the nature of the relationship between myself and the client. Psychoanalytic treatment proper uses psychoanalytic tools of understanding to effect a reorganization of the patient's inner world. Interventions related to transference, countertransference, and resistance are maximized. Behavioral change per se is of secondary importance: the analyst is as unobtrusive as possible, yet he establishes an intimate relationship with the patient. As the form of intervention moves from analysis to therapy and counseling, the focus shifts to the client's adaptation and behavior. The analyst is more actively present, though in some respects less intimately knowledgeable about the patient. Explicit use of transference, countertransference, and resistance diminishes.

To what extent can we, as analysts, move back and forth along this gradient of intervention across cases or with any one client? Do our more active interventions geared to external reality compromise a sustained focus on the inner world? Traditionally, we would answer in the affirmative. But Wallerstein's work and my own experience suggest a more flexible, effectiveness-driven conception of the work and our role. Certainly our own survival in the current workplace and culture pushes us to broaden our understanding of the analyst's identity.

I would not have undertaken this book if I did not feel that there is great value to exploring how to apply psychoanalytic principles to new populations and situations (e.g., pioneering work with borderline and narcissistic patients enriched our analytic understanding and technique immeasurably). For now, we know relatively little about how psychoanalytic understanding and technique can be used to resolve problems related to work life. As we learn more, I hope that we will also learn more about ourselves as psychoanalysts.

This book is intimately related to my learning how to be an analyst in a unique, personally compelling way. As important work projects often do, it led me to revisit some of my own early identifications, counteridentifications, needs, and defenses. It gave me an opportunity to reach for a new synthesis of these strands of my identity by combining my interest in workplace issues with a commitment to the psychoanalytic enterprise. For me personally such issues signify a work very much in progress. I hope in the future to elaborate further a clinically oriented and psychoanalytically informed approach to career development that can inform interventions across the settings of psychotherapy, career counseling, and executive coaching. I hope that readers will use the ideas, concepts, and clinical examples introduced in this book as a vehicle to rethink for themselves what constitutes a psychoanalytic approach to the problems of work life, and to consider how they might broaden their identity as psychoanalysts in a world that increasingly demands flexibility and innovation.

Introduction

The growing tendency to see work as a source of personal satisfaction has been cited as one of the most important changes in American culture since World War II (Yankelovich quoted in Lemann, 1997). Over the past 25 years, as movement from a production-oriented to a knowledge-based economy has intensified (Drucker, 1993), there has been a steady increase in the time spent at work (Schor, 1992). And it is the increasingly prominent managerial and professional sectors of the workforce whose members typically work the hardest and report the most job satisfaction. The declining role of labor unions has led to a heightened emphasis on individual ability, initiative, and satisfaction. Legislation has been passed requiring welfare recipients to work as the virtues of the work ethic have been extolled. And the dramatic increase in women in the workforce has meant that work-related concerns have reached more broadly and more deeply into the national consciousness. One sociologist has observed that the workplace has increasingly become the center of American social life (Hochschild, 1997).

Psychoanalysis, for the most part, has responded to these developments with silence. Our field has not participated in the national conversation concerning these trends in work life, and, as a result, opinion makers have not benefited from a depth psychological critique. Even more disconcertingly, as clinicians we have had little guidance regarding the implications for our work with patients. If the parameters of our patients' work lives are changing, how does this change affect the therapeutic process? Should we be dealing more with work-related issues, especially the obstacles to satisfaction in work? And, if we do not, will our clients go elsewhere for help, perhaps to vocational counselors and workplace coaches?

We can speculate about the reasons for the relative absence of a depth psychology of work. The definition of psychological health as the capacity to love *and to work* has often been attributed to Freud. In fact, this statement cannot be found anywhere in Freud's writings and comes to us by way of Erikson, one of the few psychoanalysts who discussed in depth the role of work in normal personality development. Freud considered psychoanalysis to be a cure through love (not work), and it is the ways in which sexual and affectional currents are mobilized in the transference that have made psychoanalytic treatment a powerful, radical enterprise. The more psychoanalytic treatment has come to focus on the relational bond between analyst and patient, on the vicissitudes of love and hate in the transference, the less emphasis has been placed on the work of treatment. For example, in modern technique, we have moved away from the importance Freud placed on confronting resistances in psychoanalytic treatment, when he used a model consistent with the mechanical work that typified his era.

A turning away from the structural and adaptational points of view has also contributed to the relative neglect of work in psychoanalysis. The early psychoanalytic literature on work was very much in the language of id-ego-superego, which seems antiquated and irrelevant to many current psychoanalysts. What little attention was paid to work in the psychoanalytic literature was firmly embedded in the adaptational point of view. I remember as a graduate student in the 70s being struck by the undertone of naive optimism and social conformity in Erikson's writings. My colleagues and I were more inclined to look to Marx for an understanding of work-related needs that could inform our therapeutic efforts. Many of us who came of age professionally in the 60s and 70s have been reflexively prounion and have assumed that any intrapsychic focus on effectiveness and satisfaction in work life invariably serves employers' productivity needs, not the needs of the workers.

Increased attention to the subjectivist and intersubjectivist perspectives in psychoanalysis has brought with it not only a decrease in emphasis on adaptation but a more general turning away from the givens of external reality. Certainly any notion of normative functioning tied to the world of work seems to cut against this trend in psychoanalysis. Although the *meaning* of work to the individual is of paramount importance in treatment, work is very much an activity of the concrete, external world. As such its importance is apt to be downplayed.

Creative work, which has been seen as more a function of inner life than of the outer world, has *not* been neglected by psychoanalysis.

Psychoanalysis has a rich tradition of freeing artists, writers, and performers from their inhibitions. Indeed, even when contemporary psychoanalysts address work-related issues, these issues are often tied to creative work (Socarides and Kramer, 1997). I believe that many psychoanalysts are more comfortable dealing with this inwardly focused type of enterprise, and this focus has limited our understanding of work more generally.

However, I believe that the times require us to develop a more comprehensive psychoanalytic perspective on work life. As already noted, there is evidence that work life itself is becoming more compelling and work satisfaction more important as rapid changes occur in the economy and the workplace. The boundaries between creative work and everyday work seem to be dissolving as changes occur in the tasks, roles, and authority structure of the new workplace. Changes in our own workplace, driven by the dominance of managed-care models, are influencing our relationship to our own clinical work. As we have been forced to think more in terms of therapeutic outcome and specific, behavioral interventions, we are less inclined to believe that work-related issues will take care of themselves in treatment as long as we address "deeper" issues. And, as we have experienced the anxiety and anger associated with changes in our own workplace and have been forced to rethink our professional identities, we can no longer deny the impact of work-related issues on the psyche.

In this book I hope to capture the psychological richness of work life that has so far eluded the field of psychoanalysis. The greater part of our waking lives as adults is spent working and often dealing either alone or with others with our upset about work. Our emotional involvement in work can range from great passion to profound boredom. Work can be implicated in our core hopes and wishes, and it can be a source of profound disappointment. We may strive for creative transcendence in our work, but we may also be haunted by destructive or self-destructive urges if we fall short of our goals or lose a secure place in the work world.

My goal here is to elaborate a psychoanalytic understanding of the vital, dynamic relationship a person develops with her work. My focus is on the individual—on the dimensions of work satisfaction, the barriers to healthy work functioning, and the way these barriers can be addressed in individual treatment. This is not to say that group and organizational factors are unimportant in the psychoanalytic understanding of work life. Far from it! There is, however, a long tradition of psychoanalytically oriented theory and consultation that focuses on workplace difficulties from the perspective of the group and the organization.[1] It is the individual perspective that has not been developed to anywhere near its potential.

This book is at the interface between theory and practice. Written for psychoanalytically oriented clinicians, it provides a theoretical context for understanding the individual's relationship to his work and how this develops over time. Based on material drawn largely from my clinical practice, the book is geared toward enriching the clinician's understanding of how work-related issues present themselves in individual treatment. My aim is to increase the clinician's comfort with work-related issues and to expand his repertoire of interventions in this area. Thus my focus is on expanding the existing skill set of the psychoanalytically oriented clinician.

In chapter 1, I examine the dimensions of work satisfaction from a psychoanalytic perspective. Freud viewed working as indispensable for strengthening the reality principle but was pessimistic about the capacity to obtain gratification from work. The limited psychoanalytic literature on work offers some guideposts for understanding the meaning and functions of work for the healthy personality, and I build on this literature to probe the nature of satisfaction in work and its developmental roots. Informed by a broad, multimodel perspective (Pine, 1990), I explore the different ways in which work contributes to growth of the personality. Some of the topics considered in this chapter are work and adaptation, work and the normal ego, work and self-esteem, the nature of opportunity and frustration, work and the object world, and the relationship between working and playing. I suggest there, and in later chapters, that the work–play polarity has broken down in work life much as it has in the psychoanalytic situation. Arguably, this makes work a more relevant and accessible topic for the psychoanalyst, while making him uniquely well suited to understand present-day work phenomena.

Chapter 2 is devoted to the essential connection between work life and the adult developmental process. I show how normative changes in psychological needs, capacities, and conflicts during adulthood affect work life and, in reciprocal fashion, how work life is critical in the unfolding of the personality during adulthood. This chapter is organized chronologically: starting with late adolescence and early adulthood, the key developmental tasks of adult work life are described, comprising a psychoanalytic

---

1. Much of this work has been done within the Tavistock and Group Relations tradition. Larry Hirschhorn's (1990) book *The Workplace Within* is one of the best examples of this work. See also Miller and Rice (1967) and Kets de Vries (1983).

perspective on the interaction between personality development and career.

As roles and careers become more fluid and initiative, self-direction, and self-fulfillment more centrally important in work life, psychological barriers to work functioning are becoming more salient. In chapters 3, 4, 5, and 6 I focus on some of the work-related problems most commonly encountered in the clinical situation. My approach is based on the concept of "work disturbance," which describes the characteristic patterning of functional symptoms and underlying personality dynamics of an individual's work life. Case vignettes are used to describe work inhibition, "workaholism," work diffusion (the borderline work style), and depression and disability. My intention is not to define an exhaustive typology but to enrich the clinician's sense of the phenomenology and psychodynamics of work-related problems.

Chapters 7 and 8 are devoted to treatment issues. In chapter 7, I build on the preceding discussion of work disturbance to describe how the clinician can use assessment, supportive, and exploratory interventions to treat work difficulties in psychotherapy. The importance of interventions geared to learning and mastery, as well as to self-esteem, self-object paradigms, and transference issues, are emphasized. The very place of work in the treatment process, the therapist's own values and attitudes vis-à-vis work, and the ways in which psychotherapy itself is both work and play are also discussed.

In chapter 8, I shift the focus away from psychopathology toward the issues of career development that emerge in individual psychotherapy. In this chapter I show that a psychodynamic understanding of the relationship between personality and role can point the way to effective interventions that enhance career development.

In chapter 9, I elaborate a psychoanalytic perspective on changes in the workplace. Drawing on the work of several prominent management theorists, I discuss the psychological implications of the dramatic changes that are taking place in the economy and the workplace. I show that these developments change the parameters of work life, altering the nature of the psychological demands made on the individual. People are affected differently, creating a gradient of stress and conflict as well as opportunities for growth. In the final sections of this chapter, I offer a psychoanalytic perspective on some of the specific workplace issues of greatest concern in our culture—gender differences, the balance between work and family, and the transition from welfare to work. I conclude with some comments on the psychoanalytic clinician's role vis-à-vis the changing workplace and the prospects for a specialty in work-related issues.

1

Work and Its Satisfactions

Obtaining personal satisfaction from work is a central animating force in our lives. Those who derive pleasure from their work are considered most fortunate, and those who change their lives to obtain more satisfaction from work are most admired. As clinicians, though, we understand little about the psychological dimensions of work satisfaction. If we are to help remove the emotional barriers to satisfaction in work, we need to start from a psychoanalytic understanding of work's inherent functions and satisfactions.

Work has been considered primarily a sociological concept. Work is carried out in groups or at least with reference to social groups. A society's survival depends on a viable organization of its work. Through work, the individual obtains recognition from others and establishes a place in the world. Work often holds the key to a person's status and prestige. In sociological terms, then, the basis for satisfaction (and thus for dissatisfaction) in work life seems relatively clear.

A psychoanalytic understanding of work's satisfactions has been more elusive. As clinicians, we have no models of mature working to guide us as we do varied and sophisticated models of mature loving (Bergmann, 1987; Kernberg, 1991). Lantos (1943, 1952) first suggested the possibility of "work primacy" corresponding to genital primacy, but little has been done to extend and update her concepts. As I will show later, the early psychoanalysts gave at most grudging recognition to the pleasure that can be obtained from work, thereby limiting our efforts to develop a psychoanalytic psychology of normal work life.

In this chapter I describe the most salient dimensions of a psychoanalytic understanding of normal work life. I look at the initial forays into

1

this area by the early psychoanalysts and critically evaluate the contributions of instinct theory and early ego psychology. I show that these early psychoanalytic models could not capture the richness and complexity of work life, especially as the roles, tasks, and organizational structures of the workplace have evolved. Yet, as the ideas of these pioneering psychoanalysts have faded from view, few contemporary theories of normal working have emerged.[1] I believe, though, that advances in psychoanalytic theorizing, exemplified by Pine's (1990) broad multimodel perspective, now make it possible for us to appreciate more fully the dynamic interplay between work life and personality.

Normal work life both depends on and makes possible multiple dimensions of personality development. These include not only drive and ego development, but also the evolution of ideals, self structures, object relations, and the capacity for imagination and play. I believe that the pleasure derived from working is inextricably tied to its central place in personality development. It is the essential role played by work life in the growth and development of the *total* personality that makes possible a fundamental pleasure in working, but that also makes dissatisfaction with work such a critical area of attention for the clinician.

EARLY PSYCHOANALYTIC CONCEPTION OF WORK

Freud (1930) was pessimistic about the potential for deriving pleasure from work. His few comments on work were made later in life, when he elaborated the tragic opposition between instinctual gratification and civilization. Freud posited that human civilization requires the renunciation of instinct and thus a certain degree of suffering and unhappiness. The renunciation of instinctual gratification is the cornerstone of the "compulsion to work" that human civilization requires. From this perspective the likelihood of deriving pleasure from work is slim: "And yet, as a path to happiness, work is not highly prized by men. They do not strive after it as they do after other possibilities of satisfaction. The great majority of

---

1. While Pruyser (1980) discussed the meaning of work from the different points of view of classical psychoanalysis (topographical, structural, genetic, and so forth) Czander (1993) made the first attempt to my knowledge to explore the meaning of work from the perspectives of the major theoretical schools of psychoanalysis.

people only work under the stress of necessity, and this natural human aversion to work raises most difficult social problems" (p. 80*n*).

Freud noted that work is of critical psychological value in its function of channeling instinctual energies. For Freud, all pleasure is linked to the drives, and work can be experienced as pleasurable if it becomes a vehicle of sublimated instinctual expression. While work may be resented by most because it stands in opposition to the pleasure principle, it is valuable to some for its sublimatory potential. Freud, however, seemed to think that such opportunities were limited to a small segment of the populace, mainly in the professions. Typical paradigms would be the scientist's gratification of the scopophilic instincts or the surgeon's expression of the aggressive instinct through his work.

Freud's perspective on work life reflected the realities of work in his society and concepts of mental functioning that made sense in that culture. His jaundiced view of work grew out of an era in which most of the world's economies were still primarily subsistence and agrarian. Industrial economies were based on manual labor, brute strength, and the rote activity of "making and moving things" (Drucker, 1993). A conceptualization of work in terms of the strength of the instincts and the forces mobilized to counter it reflected the dominant economic and social realities of Freud's time. As the populace has become more educated and economies become more knowledge based (Hirschhorn, 1988; Drucker, 1993), however, a much greater proportion of the workforce has become engaged in the kind of professional or quasi-professional work that in Freud's time was limited to the few. This requires a different psychoanalytic conceptualization of work life, as I will show later in this chapter and in chapter 9.

That said, I believe there is still a place for Freud's drive theory in our understanding of contemporary work life and its problems. The vicissitudes of the aggressive drive, in particular, play a critical role in work life. The aggressive instinct, in the sense it is used by ethologists to understand animal behavior, is integral to acting on the environment to obtain food and establish territory. It isn't too great a leap, I think, to see how aggression, in this sense, is identified with working.

The aggressive drive is integral to acting on the environment and thus inherent in working. It is not destructive per se, except in that it is manifested in action *without particular regard for other people*. In its sublimated and channeled forms, it takes the form of assertiveness and exploration But it is in the form of *reactive* aggression—the full panoply of frustration, anger, and destructiveness—that aggression colors work life in ways that are clinically significant.

While the role of anger in the understanding and treatment of work-related problems is discussed in more detail in subsequent chapters, I suggest that the eliciting and management of anger is an integral part of work life and the growth that can occur through working. Inasmuch as aggression mediates the struggle for survival, the aggressive drive and its derivatives are prominent in the workplace. For those with relatively intact personality functioning, or a relative freedom from problems with aggression (or both), the normal, unavoidable evoking of aggression and anger at work[2] is a stimulus to developing and channeling the aggressive urge. In these cases, aggressive urges give the individual direction and "drive" and are balanced by a regard for others. However, where the individual has a history of more frustration, deprivation, or traumatic aggression, even the normal circumstances of work life can elicit anger that disrupts goal directedness and interpersonal relationships. In these cases, anger at work becomes a focus of clinical intervention.

In the years immediately following Freud's death, psychoanalysts extended and began to modify drive theory in their attempts to understand the phenomenology and psychopathology of work life. In a series of papers in the 1940s and 1950s Barbara Lantos and Ives Hendrik specifically addressed the topic of work. Their efforts to conceptualize *normal* working in psychoanalytic terms are unique. Although subsequent analysts have addressed impairments in work functioning, few have contributed substantially to our understanding of normal working.

Lantos (1943) defined work as "the active effort of the ego, enriched during the period of learning, to get from the outside world whatever is needed for self-preservation" (p. 117). She posited a "work primacy," corresponding to genital primacy, that occurs when "the component instincts, sublimated during latency, are subsumed . . . into the productive impulse of creation" (p. 117). Lantos considered the very real phenomenon of work satisfaction in terms similar to Freud's ideas on the sublimation of instincts: "The ego effort will be the less [in working] the more pregenital instinctual energies are being used. The more these now sublimated forces succeed in ranging themselves in the purposeful structure of work, the stronger will be the basis of work in the adult's life" (p. 117). Lantos

---

2. Here I am referring to the "average, expectable" work environment. Of course, workplaces vary in the degrees to which they are characterized by aggressive behavior, whether as competitiveness, anger, or threat. There are certainly work environments characterized by a pathological degree of aggression, which not only does not serve personality growth and integration but is stressful.

further hypothesized that, since work serves self-preservation, one important consequence of normal working is the relief from fear.

In a subsequent paper, Lantos (1952) elaborated her understanding of work pleasure. Drawing on Hendrik's (1943) concept of the "mastery instinct," she added the idea of the ego's reaction of pleasure in achievement to that of sublimated instinctual energies linked to working. Elaborating on the role of the superego in work life, Lantos suggested that the motive of self-preservation takes the form of superego pressure. She emphasized the balance between sublimated instinctual energy and pleasure in achievement, on one hand, and the pressure of the superego, on the other, as the key to mature (and pleasurable) working:

> Libidinal and achievement-pleasure, stemming from the instinctual forces and all the ego-skills which are used, should be, usually, in excess of the tension which is felt, whenever work is done under superego-pressure. We might say that the specific work pleasure is the relief from this tension, the harmony between ego and superego [p. 442].

Hendrik (1943), writing shortly after Hartmann (1939), argued that the ego develops autonomously from the drives, made a key contribution to the development of ego psychology by positing the existence of the "instinct to master." According to Hendrik, the instinct to master is an inborn drive the aim of which is "to control or alter a piece of the environment, an ego-alien situation, by the skilful use of perceptual, intellectual, and motor techniques. . ." (p. 314). The pleasure associated with the instinct to master derives from the successful carrying out of a function and is not secondary to the sexual instincts, as Freud and then Lantos had emphasized. Work is the primary means by which the instinct to master gains expression, and pleasure in working derives from the instinct to master.

White (1963), building on Hendrik's ideas, postulated the existence of an independent ego energy termed the "effectance" motive. White suggested that acting on the environment, producing effects on it and changes in it, leads to "a feeling of efficacy which *is a primitive biological endowment* that is as basic as the satisfactions that accompany feeding or sexual gratification . . ." (p. 35). The feeling of efficacy that derives from effective interaction with the environment is inherently pleasurable.

Thus, White's ideas have important implications for our understanding of work-derived pleasure. According to this line of thinking, pleasure in work stems from the exercise and growth of component ego functions involved in the performance of a job, as well as from the more goal-related sense of a job well done.

I believe that the ideas of Hendrik and White are most applicable to understanding the critical role of challenge in work life. The instinct to master or the effectance motive propels us toward challenging work. Most of us seek the optimal level of challenge in work: not so little as to lead to boredom nor so much as to lead to an inordinate degree of frustration. A challenging job is based on having new experiences, encountering new sectors of the environment that need to be controlled, altered, or influenced in some way. It requires the person to "stretch," to use new skills and abilities or to refine those she already has. The exercise of these functions and the mastery of the environment associated with an optimally challenging job are pleasurable. Conversely, the lack of challenge in jobs that are repetitive or too easy, blocks the instinct to master. In these cases, a person is liable to experience a sense of depression and malaise and to feel that personality growth in a fundamental sense is not occurring.

WORK AND THE EGO

Jahoda (1966) suggested that work provides an important means by which the pleasure and the reality principles are synthesized. Work not only ties a person to reality but offers the means by which he can obtain uniquely adult sources of pleasure. Thus, the increased knowledge of reality and the growth of component ego functions obtained through work serve the end-state of pleasurable reward. The refinement of ego functions helps map the pathways to achievement and attendant gratification. In this sense, the pleasure and reality principles are mutually reinforcing.

Mature working requires, and at the same time facilitates, the ongoing development of such ego functions as focal attention and concentration, judgment, reality testing, and planning and anticipation. Hendrik, White, and other ego psychologists have taught us that the exercise and growth of these functions in interaction with the environment are inherently pleasurable. I would like to discuss some of the specific ways in which these component ego functions are linked to working.

The ability to focus attention on a task forms a critical substrate for mature working. Developing the capacity to maintain focus and see a complex task through to completion in the face of competing demands for attention is an essential part of working. This means that one must prioritize her efforts and learn to manage her time effectively. The more complex and demanding the job, the more demands are made on the individual's ego to carry out these functions. At the same time, deficits in the capacity for focal attention can make even a seemingly ordinary job inordinately stressful.

Work life provides continuous opportunities for the exercise and development of judgment. Jaques (1965) has suggested that the level of one's work is a function of the discretion and judgment exercised on the job. Jobs vary in the relative importance of the prescribed and discretionary components, and people vary in the relative weighting of those components that they are comfortable with and seek out. A job that is right for a person "carries a challenge to judgment and discretion" (p. 129) without stimulating excessive doubt and uncertainty.

The refinement of reality testing is at the core of mature working. Freud (1930) noted that, in addition to offering opportunities for displacement of the drives, work plays a critical role in binding the individual more closely to reality. Subsequently, Holmes (1965) hypothesized that, for a given individual, work serves primarily either the function of drive expression or that of enhancing the tie to reality. In the latter case, he suggested that work experience should be seen in terms of the opportunities it provides for the development of the self-evaluative, planning, and *reality orienting* functions.

Work, then, is one of the most important ways by which we know the world around us; it is based on the progressive differentiation of external reality from wishful fantasies. At work, we try to see the world the way it is and to accommodate to changing circumstances. We constantly ask ourselves if our old habits and ways of working fit the current circumstances.[3] As the pace of change and complexity of information to be processed increase in the contemporary workplace, a premium is placed on this reality-testing function. Doing a job well under variable and complex conditions depends on a person's expanding his scope of understanding of the external world.

An important manifestation of reality testing in work life is the ability to identify and take advantage of opportunity. Openness to new experience in concert with good reality testing helps determine one's relationship to opportunity. Degrees of ego strength are evident in the abilities to

---

3. Reality testing in this respect can be seen as not only an individual, but also a group and organizational, function. For a work group or an organization to function effectively, it must constantly test the cognitive maps, traditions, and feelings that define its culture against the changing realities of its environment.

perceive, make sense of, and develop opportunity in vital interaction with the environment. At the same time, ego development depends on a "good enough" (Winnicott, 1950) or "average expectable" (Hartmann, 1939) work environment, relatively free of deprivation and trauma.

The management of risk in work life, like the relationship to opportunity, could be considered a higher order ego function that helps define the contours of one's relationship to the surrounding world. The importance of risk in work life has been emphasized by Hirschhorn (1988): "Work entails risks, which are experienced psychologically as threats that must be aggressively met, contained, and ultimately transformed into challenges and opportunities" (p. 33). Meeting risks is exciting and a major source of pleasure. Hirschhorn reminds us, however, that conflicts over aggression in particular can lead to withdrawal from risk, with a resulting impairment in task performance and enfeeblement of the sense of opportunity.

Effectiveness at work requires planning and anticipation. Goal achievement depends on the capability for delay and multistep planning. It is not enough to reality test current environmental circumstances; anticipating changing circumstances is an increasingly important part of work life. The ability to employ reality testing and anticipation, as well as a sophisticated time sense to discern patterns and trends, is increasingly important in the complex, rapidly changing, information-based workplace.

The current emphasis on "vision" in organizational life suggests that the development of higher order ego functions is linked to the requirements of the contemporary workplace. Work life has become the primary arena in which the individual develops the ability for strategic thinking. Strategic thinking is abstract, future oriented, and action linked. It is an essential part of both an individual's career and a group's and organization's functioning. The concept of "vision" adds elements of imagination and a deeper knowledge of oneself and one's development to the conventional notion of strategic thinking. While vision is often thought of as a function of leadership, it can also develop in a collaborative context.

Work bears an important relationship to the synthetic and integrative functions of the ego. Especially as workplaces become characterized by rapid change and complex input from multiple sources, a premium is placed on being able to synthesize data and see the "big picture." Effective work functioning draws on the coordination of ego functions to assess constantly changing situations and plan a course of action consistent with a person's skills, values, and position.

Erikson (1950) underscored the importance of work for the development of the integrative function he termed "ego identity." He described the ways in which vocational choice during late adolescence synthesizes ego abilities, talents, and self- and object representations in a unique identity constituting fashion (Erikson, 1958, 1968, 1969). Erikson had a ready grasp of how work provides a means by which an individual is known by others and better knows herself. Work and career, important constituents of psychosocial identity, give the person both a sense of being valued by the community at large and opportunities for authentic self-expression.

WORK AND THE SELF

Freud's perspective on work was based on the implacable opposition between the superego and the drives—work requires the imposition of adult injunctions and prohibitions on our childish natures. Lantos (1952), elaborating on Freud's ideas, wrote that "aggression becomes . . . internalized and used by the superego to make the ego exert all its instinctual resources and submit to hardship and boredom . . . what is felt as the urge to work is the voice of the superego" (p. 442).

But the picture of work and the superego painted by the early psychoanalysts oversimplifies the situation. To the extent that we are driven by our instincts, work does indeed require the kind of prohibition represented by superego pressure. There *is* an element of force, coercion, and compulsion to work life for many people. But, to the extent that we are motivated by needs for self-definition and self-cohesion, values and ideals play an important part in our work lives.

The articulation of mature, workable values is indeed a critical function of the superego. The superego's implication in work life is not limited to the injunction to "work and don't play." How we work and what we are willing to do under different circumstances in the workplace serve a critical function in defining our own values. Indeed, the workplace is a critical domain in which we define what we stand for. The ability to bring an appropriate degree of aggression to bear in expressing and carrying out our values is a hallmark of mature working. Careers are animated, in large part, by the striving to harmonize the exigencies of the job and the workplace with a sense of one's deeper values.

The experience of working in harmony with one's values is commonly a source of pride and satisfaction. Patients in therapy, however, frequently grapple with the feeling that their work lives, no matter how successful, are not consistent with their values. A central part of work life is behaving in a way that is felt to express one's core values, even in the face of considerable pressure to act otherwise. By core values I mean not only such common virtues as honesty, respectfulness, openness, and the like, although these are important. I am referring also to the refinement of work-related values that occurs over the course of a career and that defines success for a person. Work-related success is always a very personal affair, even if it is constituted partly by commonly acknowledged monetary and status indicators. For example, one person may forgo an assignment that seems to be the quickest route to the top of her company—thereby risking the displeasure of the leadership circle—in order to affirm the value she places on doing research and policy work in her field. Another person may have to wrestle with whether to accept a very lucrative contract if it means compromising his artistic freedom and ability to do innovative, even controversial work. These are the kinds of decisions that shape a career and that give one an all-important sense of having defined and expressed one's values amidst the flux and pressure of the workplace.

While a person may be *pushed* to work by the prohibiting superego, he is *led* by his ideals and the need for self-expression. Coinciding with a shift in emphasis from the obedience and rule following at work that was characteristic of Freud's era to the quest for meaningful work that typifies our own, a contemporary understanding of work is best informed not only by concepts related to the superego but also by those pertaining to the ego ideal.

Post-Freudian developments in psychoanalysis have led to a fuller understanding of the functions of the ego ideal. Whereas the superego refers to parental prohibitions that become expressed as conscience, the ego ideal represents the sum of positive identifications with the parental images and constitutes a model to which the person attempts to conform (Piers and Singer, 1953; Laplanche and Pontalis, 1973). The genesis of the ego ideal has been traced to the human infant's helplessness and the megalomaniacal character of infantile narcissism (Reich, 1960; Piers and Singer, 1953; Chasseguet-Smirgel, 1985). Early strivings to become like the protective and confirming parents are forerunners of the ego ideal. The child's pride in his own evolving effectiveness becomes linked to the idealization of the parents and shapes the content of the ego ideal. The child's model of his own growth and attainment of an environmental niche becomes based on a progressively broader understanding of the adult world, including the world of work. Images of his parents at work become amalgamated with the young child's nascent efforts at "work" in the home and the parents' reactions to them.

The content of the ego ideal pertaining to work reflects the child's developmental level as well as the unique aspects of her personality and her family environment. Initially, the young child's models of work life are little more than imitations of her parents—the youngster dressing up in her parents' clothing to "go to work." Work itself is understood either in concrete terms or in terms of glamor and heroism.

Erikson (1950) called latency the "age of industry" and believed that the latency-aged child's activities provide a basis for mature working in adulthood. In learning, practicing, and playing out preferred modes of acting on the environment, the child develops more refined schemas of work in adulthood. The all-important involvement in group activities, whether in the schoolroom or on the playground, gives him a much truer sense of adult work activity. He begins to articulate career goals that explicitly relate to the kind of person he sees himself as and wants to become. A better understanding of the parents' work roles, and especially their feelings about their work lives, becomes incorporated into the child's ego ideal.

Idealizations intensify during adolescence, and the growth and reworking of the ego ideal help lead the child into the wider world. By late adolescence, ideals normatively assume a more realistic, guiding function for life beyond the family of origin. At this time, however, the effects of pathological ego ideal development on work life may become apparent for the first time. Blos (1985) noted cases of the "infantilism of the work principle" during adolescence, in which ideals pertaining to work become infused with either crude, infantile grandiosity or with despair and cynicism.

In adulthood, the ego ideal is, in part, a repository of images and fantasies associated with successful working. The degree to which a person feels that he is living up to this model of work life determines his self esteem and thus the amount of pleasure derived from working. The refinement, even the redefinition of ideals connected to work life, is a critical component of adult development, as will be discussed further in chapter 2. The fuller articulation of coherent, realistic, yet highly personal ideals is an important part of all work-related interventions and has significant benefits for improved self-esteem.

Kohut's self psychology offers a somewhat different perspective on the centrality of ideals and self-esteem in development and psychopathology. Kohut placed great emphasis on the affirmation of the self through productive and creative activity and showed how the devotion to meaningful work goals strengthens the self and gives a person a feeling of being alive, real, and worthwhile.

Kohut posited a developmental progression from merger with the mirroring selfobject to merger with the idealized selfobject. Satisfactory experience with the former leads to the consolidation of a nuclear grandiose-exhibitionistic self that is the locus of ambition, while optimal merger with the idealized selfobject leads to the formation of guiding ideals and the capacity for true goal directedness. Psychological health, the establishment of a cohesive self, depends on the integration, specific for each person, of these two poles of the self via *nuclear talents and skills*. The "flow of actual psychological activity" from nuclear ambitions via nuclear talents and skills to nuclear idealized goals constitute "a person's basic pursuits toward which he is 'driven' by his ambitions and 'led' by his ideals." (Kohut, 1977, p. 180).

In very specific terms, through a number of case illustrations, Kohut showed how defects in the early idealization of the parents (especially the father) lead to the absence of guiding ideals and the enfeeblement of the self vis-à-vis work. Analysis and working through of the idealizing transference can lead to articulation of realizable goals and the revitalization of work life. Kohut strongly believed that "rehabilitation" of this sector of the personality can compensate for early failures in the mirroring selfobject, thereby constituting an analytic cure. In other words, *even when early empathic failures are not fully worked through*, the strengthening of internalized ideals can result in the increased creative and productive activity that is the hallmark of a vital, cohesive self.

Thus, when it comes to the satisfactions of work life, there are important commonalities among Erikson's concept of psychosocial identity, Piers and Singer's ego ideal, and Kohut's nuclear self. All these theorists underscore the importance of authentic self-expression in work life and the developmental roots of this experience. The synthesis of individual talents and skills with values and goals to create a guiding model of oneself at work is not only a major developmental achievement, it is also a source of pleasure and self-esteem residing in the deepest levels of the psyche.

WORK AND THE OBJECT WORLD

Jaques (1960) showed that the seeming impersonality of task performance can be understood in object relations terms. The processes by which a person sets objectives, overcomes obstacles, and creates opportunities at work can be linked, in the unconscious, to ways in which she has established and worked through relationships with primary objects.

From Jaques's Kleinian perspective, an objective is an "object-to-be," which has to be brought into being or created. Obstacles to achieving the objective are identified with "bad objects, bad impulses, and bad parts of the self" (p. 360). Thus overcoming obstacles to achieve an objective constitutes a reparation and is an important way of working through the infantile depressive position to facilitate personality growth.

Writing from a similar point of view, Hirschhorn (1988; 1996, personal communication) has described the reparative functions of normal working. He postulated an equation between completing a task and "making objects whole" in the psychoanalytic sense. Task completion enables the individual or the group to counteract inner feelings of fragmentation associated with the unconscious sense of badness or destructiveness. Completing a task offers a means of restoring the outer world and, in so doing, restoring a personal sense of wholeness.

The experience of obstacle writ large is failure. Failure is ubiquitous in work life, and the way that failure is represented intrapsychically is probably the most important indicator of the maturity of one's relationship to work. Failure can be the signal to begin a search for new resources, both internally and externally. To the extent that failure at a task eventuates in reflection, learning, and the formulation of new objectives, it can become an important source of personality growth in adulthood. At the same time, the identification of failures with what Jaques (1960) called the bad aspects of the self can have a corrosive effect on the personality.

Thus, obstacles, setbacks, and failure in work life elicit negative affects that are unconsciously identified with childhood experiences of helplessness and the depressive feelings that accompanied them. Mastering and integrating these affective experiences through work becomes an important source of personality growth in adulthood. At the same time, the experience of opportunity through work life provides the ambience or background of a positive object relationship in which the self at work can develop.

Freud (1930) observed that "no other technique for the conduct of life attaches the individual so firmly to reality as laying emphasis on work; for his work at least gives him a secure place in a portion of reality, in the human community" (p. 80). The workplace requires a kind of mapping of the social world. In contrast to the ambiguity and high intensity of intimate relationships, the workplace is built on instrumental and relatively more structured relationships. The experience of being part of a well-functioning work group can be deeply satisfying, and it may actually be the preferred mode of relating for some people.

Being able to work effectively with other people is increasingly at a premium in today's workplace. As I discuss in more detail in chapter 9, the less the workplace is based on hierarchy and routine tasks and the more it is centered on ad hoc projects and networks of communication, the more management of interpersonal relationships becomes important. Since the form and content of these relationships are less rigidly dictated, skills are needed to generate and maintain them effectively. Sensitivity to differences in motives, goals, and personality style make it possible to influence other people and situations more effectively. Thus, work offers myriad opportunities for understanding other people, and increasingly it requires such understanding.

Being recognized as a member of a social group is a deeply rooted species need that can be satisfied through work life. Recognition for one's contribution to the work group, however, may not be forthcoming in the particular form or at the particular pace at which it is expected. This disjunction creates a normal tension in work life; it requires a constant reworking and balancing of narcissistic and group needs. This is the crucible in which much interpersonal learning occurs in the workplace.

Thus, mature working requires the individual to find her place in the social group. Doing so entails an increasingly refined appreciation of the reality of other people in relation to the accomplishment of an objective, for example, an appraisal of their abilities to either obstruct or facilitate. It also means understanding the realities of both leadership and followership. Although workplace hierarchies may be flattening, the reality of power in work relationships will never disappear and must be actively managed as part of mature working. Integration into the work group also requires empathy for others' needs without losing sight of one's own values and goals, even under the pressure of rapid change and multiple demands. In a very important sense, then, work life both depends on and at the same time fosters self–other differentiation.

Finally, success and satisfaction in work depend on the successful management of one's own aggression. The more narcissistic a person, the more the realities of other people's needs and goals can be experienced as frustrating obstacles, leading to anger and hostility. Mistrust, envy, contempt, entitlement, vengefulness, and outright hostility may have their roots in early experience but find ready, highly personalized targets in the workplace. Adverse conditions may lead to chronic complaining and resentment toward others rather than constructive action. Authority relationships may become suffused with feelings of humiliation and rage. To the extent that frustration and anger can be worked through and subordinated to the task and the group effort required, the individual is able to move toward higher levels of object relatedness.

WORK AND PLAY

Lantos's (1943) original metapsychology of work was organized around what she felt were fundamental distinctions among work, learning, and play. She argued that in play what is done is done for its own sake. Learning is undertaken to acquire the ability for self-preservation, and work is activity that is undertaken not for its own sake but, rather, serves the end of self-preservation. More recently, Plaut (1979) drew a similar distinction between work and play along the lines of instrumentality. He defined play as "a form of action that is pleasurable, freely chosen, intrinsically complete, and noninstrumental" while work is "an activity producing something useful or valuable" (pp. 220–221).

The relationship, in developmental terms, between work and play has been a subject of some controversy in the psychoanalytic literature. Some authors have traced a direct line between play in childhood and work in adulthood while others have postulated separate childhood origins for work.

Anna Freud (1965) described a developmental line from play to work. She emphasized the progression from autoerotic play and play with the mother of the symbiotic period to later investment in the toys and games that come to represent the external world. The capacity to use play to move from narcissism to cathexis of the external world is thus an important precursor of the capacity to work. According to Anna Freud, the ability to play changes into the ability to work with the maturation of the ego—the growing capacities to control impulses, tolerate frustration, carry out plans, and defer pleasure. This development first becomes evident during the latency period (Erikson's, 1950, "Age of Industry") when work and play are beginning to be differentiated as spheres of activity but are still closely allied and mutually strengthening.

Furman (1997), challenging Anna Freud's ideas, differentiates the aims and functions of work and play even during childhood. Furman argues that the capacity to work is rooted in the young child's emerging capacity for self-care. She emphasizes the importance of early parent–child caretaking interactions in making the child's self-care, and later the adult's working, nonconflictual and pleasurable.

Kramer (1977) has added yet another perspective, linking the child's learning to the adult's working. Like others who have considered learning the child's work, Kramer postulates that conflicts and inhibitions in learning during childhood can eventuate in adult work difficulties. (This point of view is in accord with the clinical material described in an earlier paper [Axelrod, 1994], in which childhood learning problems seemed to be precursors of a particular kind of adult work difficulty.) Kramer describes a case in which family secrets give rise to conflicts about knowing and problems in learning during childhood and later, in adulthood, to a work inhibition.

I believe that the sharp distinctions among work, learning, and play that formed the basis of Lantos's (1952) metapsychology are simplistic. They entail a focus on aim or goal as the defining element of human activity and give relatively short shrift to process. A developmental perspective helps us understand the interconnectedness of playing, learning, and working. If there is truly a developmental line from play to work (A. Freud, 1965), then wouldn't we expect that some of the pleasure associated with play during childhood would be present in adult work life? Or, if the developmental line is one from self-care (embedded in tender contact and guidance of the parent–child interaction) to work, then don't we arrive at a much richer understanding of work than just activity serving self-preservation?

Furthermore, the conception of work used by Lantos and Plaut is outmoded, rendering their metapsychological schemes even less valid. Lantos's theorizing, like Freud's before her, is implicitly based on work as a sequence of rote, repetitive tasks performed under the duress of the superego. While such work is still a prominent part of our economy, the current picture is much more variegated. In a knowledge-based economy (Drucker, 1993), formulating objectives and developing projects require vision and imagination. Work groups may engage in aspects of collective daydreaming and play with different solutions to a given problem.

Lantos, Hendrik, Plaut, and others, in making sharp distinctions between work and play, did not consider the creative work of the artist. I believe, though, that shifts in the economy have blurred the boundaries between everyday work and creative work, making it imperative that we consider play with symbols an important part of present-day work life. In this regard, D. W. Winnicott's ideas on play and creativity have real bearing on present day work life. Winnicott (1971) located the "area of playing" in the potential space that was originally between the mother and the baby and that belongs exclusively to neither inner psychic reality nor external reality. In the play area, "the child manipulates external phenomena in the service of the dream and invests chosen external phenomena with dream meaning and feeling" (p. 51). In this sense, the young child, absorbed in a world of play, begins to find a way to join his early omnipotent fantasies to the world of actual objects. Might the process described by Winnicott be another developmental antecedent of working in the postindustrial milieu? Where strict hierarchization of authority and segmentation of tasks is no longer required, the expression of omnipotence in the playspace described by Winnicott may have adaptive counterparts in the "workspace." I believe that the more we see work as a creative alteration of the external world that allows, even requires, pleasurable self-expression, the more we will see the capacity for playing as an essential part of work life.

2

Work and Adult Development

I n chapter 1 I discussed the role of work in healthy personality functioning from a cross-sectional perspective. The focus was on the psychology of work life at one point in time. Yet work has a time trajectory. The very concept of a career, of work life that develops and has coherence over time, has become more prevalent in recent decades. In this chapter I take a developmental perspective, focusing on the adaptation to work as a dynamic process over time. I explore the interaction between a person's evolving needs and capacities in adulthood and the parameters of work life. I believe that a person's relationship to her work, shaped by underlying personality development, changes over time. The tasks and central themes of the different epochs of adulthood put their stamp on work life during any particular period. At the same time, work is a critical source for the expanding capacities of the self during that period.

The chronological perspective on work life that is elaborated in this chapter straddles the career development and psychoanalytic approaches to personality in adulthood. My emphasis is not on the specifics of career development per se as described by Super (1957) and others, for I am less interested in the dynamics of career development than in how the defining characteristics of early and middle adulthood, understood in psychoanalytic terms, influence work life. Naturally, there is much individual variability in how the relationship to work unfolds during adulthood. But there are certain normative tasks or demands of different epochs of adulthood that give shape to work life for many people. Thus, in this chapter, I outline a kind of *ideal type analysis*—a way of understanding the stages of adult work life that is valid in the aggregate and that provides a framework for approaching clinical cases.

The adult developmental perspective (see Neugarten, 1968; Gould, 1972; Levinson et al., 1978; Colarusso and Nemiroff, 1981) that informs this chapter emphasizes the dynamic, constantly changing nature of the organism *throughout the life span*. From our study of development during childhood we are accustomed to thinking of psychological development as being tied to biological maturation. Indeed, Ross (1994) has argued that the term adaptation is more appropriate than "development" to describe change during adulthood for this reason. I disagree with Ross and believe that personality changes corresponding to the life cycle reflect core human needs no less for not being tied to biological maturation. This is not to minimize the importance of biological phenomena (e.g., childbearing, menopause, aging) in precipitating changes in the adult personality. Rather, it is to emphasize that psychological development, defined, according to Webster, as "the gradual advance or growth through progressive changes," occurs in a lawful fashion even if the biological substrate is one of decline rather than maturation.

The adult developmental perspective is based on the fact that experience in adulthood is not reducible to factors in childhood even if the latter have had a decisive effect on personality formation. Experiences in adulthood have their own imperatives that offer their own opportunities for personality growth. Adult experience can lead to the reworking of earlier conflicts and deficits or can render them less disruptive of personality functioning.

Thus, as I show in the clinical section of this book, the adult developmental and genetic perspectives on work life are complementary and often mutually enriching. The problems of work life often present themselves and are most readily understood as adult developmental crises and tasks. For example, initial problems in choosing and committing to a career path often reflect difficulties in the "third separation-individuation" and identity formation processes of early adulthood; a stalled career at midlife may be a function of the typical anxieties of this period. Understanding a problem in these terms can itself lead to a therapeutic result. Or exploring the phenomenology of the patient's work life can serve as a departure point for understanding childhood developmental issues. I am suggesting that either approach, or some combination of the two, is valid in psychodynamic terms and can have potent therapeutic effects. I hope that the adult developmental approach to work life described in this chapter will be seen as a valuable addition to our typical emphasis on childhood developmental factors in addressing clinical problems.

ENTERING THE ADULT WORLD

Occupational Choice

Beginning in *Childhood and Society* (1950), and continuing in his later biographical studies (1958, 1968, 1969), Erik Erikson elaborated on his central contribution to contemporary thought—the concept of ego identity as a developmental achievement. For Erikson (1950) the achievement of psychosocial identity in late adolescence and early adulthood hinges on a choice of career that represents the integration of "all identifications with the vicissitudes of the libido, with the aptitudes developed out of endowment, and with the opportunities offered in social roles" (p. 161). In his case studies, Erikson described how a young person may have to struggle with strongly conflicting identifications, or with disparities between his own skills and talents and what is expected by the family and the culture, to arrive at an occupational choice that bears the stamp of personal authenticity.

In her case study of a college student's career choice as it unfolded in individual psychotherapy, Medalie (1976) applied and extended Erikson's ideas about psychosocial identity and career choice. Medalie was able to follow the *process* of her patient's career choice from an initial choice driven by neurotic identifications and counteridentifications to one that bore the stamp of ego autonomy and synthesized his various needs and abilities.

This young man's initial choice of a career as a chemist was maladaptive for three reasons. First, it represented a reaction against a verbal facility that was still bound up with oral-dependent longings. Second, it expressed a fantasy of achieving a masculine identity through the "manly enterprise" of science. And, third, it expressed a flight from the interpersonal world toward the safety of formulae and rules. As her patient's therapy progressed, however, it became apparent that Medalie's patient didn't like this work and was not particularly good at it. He had to free himself from the unconscious family dictum that "to work is to suffer" and discover (at first through hobbies) that he could pleasurably engage his interests. The growing awareness that he could work pleasurably for himself, not masochistically for his mother, furthered the differentiation of his interests. Medalie's patient became interested in organizational psychology, a field that blended his real verbal/conceptual abilities with the rigor of a more scientific enterprise. Identification with the therapist and a need to master the complex "organizational dynamics" of his family also helped determine the choice.

Thus, Medalie was able to develop a psychoanalytic understanding of her patient's career interests, both maladaptive and adaptive. Her case report showed how Erikson's ideas could be applied and extended to career issues in the clinical setting. Indeed, she convincingly demonstrated how progress in treatment was intertwined with the differentiation of the patient's interests and eventual commitment to a career that became a form of genuine self-expression.

Erikson's work on identity remains a seminal contribution to the psychology of occupational choice. The choice of an occupation represents an impressive synthesis of defensive style and sublimatory capacity, counteridentification and identification, even a creative working through of early trauma. Erikson's concept of identity formation, however, suffers from a kind of teleological fallacy—all the individual's conflicts and provisional choices are subsumed under the ultimate vocational choice that so well meshes self and society. In reality, in today's complex, fast-changing society, the process of finding such a niche is usually neither simple nor accomplished once and for all. From our clinical work, we know that people may struggle for years, especially during their 20s, to reconcile a provisionally chosen occupational course with other choices that are longed for and dreamed about. They may need more guidance than they did in a simpler economy 50 years ago in making a vocational choice that truly synthesizes personality and social role.

Levinson et al.'s (1978) concept of the "personal dream" further clarifies the process of occupational choice and its relationship to identity formation. The authors described the personal dream as being initially "a vague sense of self-in-adult-world. It has the quality of a vision, an imagined possibility that generates excitement and vitality" (p. 91). During the entry into adulthood, the young person forms and begins to find ways to live out the vocational dream. Conflict may arise between the wishful self-representations of the dream and the realities of the person's skills, talents, and environmental opportunities. Over time, the resolutions of these conflicts can lead to modifications in the dream and to more specific, personal ways of living it out. Throughout adult life, the dream plays an important organizing and guiding function in work life.

Levinson et al.'s personal dream is another way of thinking about the ego ideal as it applies to work life. In chapter 1, the ego ideal was defined as a wishful self-image, a model of the self based on positive identifications with parents and other figures that the person attempts to live up to. Levinson et al. draw our attention to the point that the ego ideal is not just a static structure but is experienced as a guiding vision of one's work life and career. How that dream is lived out over time gives form and content to one's self-esteem vis-à-vis work life.

Confusion about career choice and conflict over ambition itself are common issues in the treatment of young adult patients. During this period, the personal dream is untested and frequently vague while sheer ambition is often intense. The young person has an intuitive sense of her own strength, determination, and talents but is just beginning to develop skills in the real world and has relatively little sense of others' needs and motives vis-à-vis work. She wants, above all else, to prove herself and to be taken seriously by her elders but fears that she doesn't have what it takes.

Oscillations in self-esteem are characteristic of this period as the pleasure of beginning to make one's way in the world alternates with the real limitations of being a novice. Fluctuations between feelings of omnipotence and morbid self-doubt are not uncommon as the young person is deeply involved in sorting out fantasies about his work identity. The status of beginner at work may be especially difficult for some, with resentment dominating their day-to-day experience of work.

Relationships with Authority, Mentors, and Intimates

The feelings of omnipotence that accompany the young person's initial forays beyond the family of origin into the world of work can bring her into conflict with the authority and structure of the workplace. Entering the world of work during her 20s, the young person must learn to harness the high energy and often unbridled ambition of this period. On the job, she learns to manage aggression by developing work habits and identifying with group goals. However, anger and frustration may be aroused by the authority structure of the workplace. Relationships to bosses are qualitatively different from the relationships to teachers during the previous period. People of authority in the workplace may be relatively unconstrained in their exercise of power and typically have a more immediate effect on the young person's survival. The novice worker must learn to contend with the exercise of authority, legitimate or corrupt, benign or malignant.

Transferences to figures of authority in the workplace are typically quite raw for young adults in the novice phase of work life. The young worker, who does not yet have a well-developed sense of his own skills and therefore his own worth in the workplace, may feel that the boss can make or break him. The feelings of vulnerability and fear, frustration and anger, can rekindle old feelings of being abused and exploited. Under the worst circumstances, a kind of developmental arrest occurs, in which the young adult continually sees himself in the victim role vis-à-vis authority in the workplace. In other cases, he tries either to work in isolation or to work at low-level jobs to avoid putting himself "on the line" with people in authority.

Experience with a mentor offers a potent countervailing force to experiences with indifferent and intimidating figures of authority in the workplace. The young person in her 20s, having traveled only a short distance from the family of origin, has a special need for someone to admire and model herself after, who in turn takes a special interest in her. The mentor typically shows the young person not only how to do the job well, but how to do it in a special way that is personally compelling for the mentee. The mentor also confirms the novice's sense of being a valued, legitimate member of an enterprise. In both respects, the relationship with the mentor helps the young person reshape her relationship with the inner images of authority from the past.

How universal is the mentoring relationship? The salience of mentoring may well vary according to the field of endeavor and may be especially important where disadvantage or inexperience are characteristic of a particular group in the workplace.[1] Mentoring is itself a highly variable phenomenon. The mentoring relationship may be more or less direct, in some instances characterized more by modeling and in other cases more by conferring promotions and prestige. People also vary in their need for and receptivity to a mentoring relationship. Some young adults effectively develop their careers as loners; others seem particularly adept at cultivating relationships with those in power. Conflicts over dependency may be evident in the avoidance of a mentoring relationship or in a highly dependent relationship to the mentor.

The mentoring relationship is by definition a time-limited one. It serves an important developmental function that typically ends as the young person moves from novice to master. How the mentoring relationship ends is very important for clinicians to understand. The mentor's role in the young person's life may change, or the relationship may terminate altogether. In some cases, ending a mentoring relationship may become a stormy affair that leaves real emotional scars. The mentoring relationship, built as it is on experiences of idealization and then deidealization, plays a critical role in the growth of self-structures during adulthood.

---

1. In such instances, a formal mentoring program can be effective, although some element of informality or free choice on the part of the young person increases the likelihood that the mentoring program will meet the *psychological* needs of the young person.

Work-based friendships, like the relationship to a mentor, provide an important source of personal recognition to the young worker. Friendships with fellow workers that develop during the 20s are typically more intensely personal than the colleagueships that are characteristic of the next decade. These relationships are very important in helping the young person bridge the gaps experienced between the personal self and the work self. The normative impersonality and instrumentality of the workplace, more difficult for some than for others, is mitigated in important ways by mentorships and workplace friendships.

The stress involved in assuming the instrumental role of worker can lead some young adults to try to obtain a kind of personal recognition in the workplace that is neither appropriate nor forthcoming. However, in some cases the experience of a split between the personal self and the work self may become a motivating force central to the vocational dream. It may lead to a sharpening of the person's values and to a clearer sense of direction. For example, wishing to provide a better synchrony between the personal self and the work self, the person may either start his own venture or take measures over time to "humanize" his workplace.

Achieving a stable work role in early adulthood frequently coincides with establishing an intimate love relationship (Erikson, 1950). There is no fixed sequence in accomplishing these two tasks, but their reciprocal effects are of defining importance in the young person's development. Levinson et al. (1978) emphasized the important role of the partner in sharing and supporting a young person's vocational dream. The intimate partner can bestow a kind of recognition on the young person as *both* lover and worker that facilitates personality integration. By recognizing the person's aspirations and goals, the intimate partner validates them and often gives them further specificity. The development of an intimate partnership can give focus to ambitions that were diffuse and conflictual. Most important, the capacities for mutuality and empathy that develop in an intimate relationship can lead to a better appreciation of the interpersonal world of the workplace. The dialogue between lovers about work-related matters can be a key to better work functioning, and is a phenomenon that I believe should be further studied.

THE ERA OF MASTERY

Levinson et al. (1978) proposed a shift around age 30 to a more serious commitment to one's work and a stronger identification with one's field of endeavor. This shift often means consciously taking stock of one's work life, accompanied by revision or fuller articulation of one's vocational dream. It is not uncommon at this time for a person to decide on a subspecialty, to strike out in a different direction within his field of endeavor, or even to change fields entirely. The common element in all three is the weighing of alternative courses of action and the conscious decision to "take the next step." As a result, the person becomes better able to articulate the importance of what he does, the ways in which the specific job contributes to a larger enterprise and to the general well-being of society.[2]

During this period, the person gauges the degree of her ambition and focuses on advancement. Her dream becomes more closely associated with achieving a particular position in the work world and is linked to certain types of material and status rewards. The vocational dream takes shape as a "personal enterprise" that often dominates work life in the 30s and beyond. The personal enterprise is a specific program for action in the world of work that encompasses an understanding of the person's vocational strengths, areas of potential contribution, and the means of achieving goals. It marks an important development in work life in that it is both future-oriented *and* specific.

Work life in the 30s is characterized first and foremost by the refinement and exercise of skills. The worker in his 30s is close to technical innovations and not yet too taken up with administrative demands that he is his field's state of the art practitioner. With the benefit of considerable experience he is adept at distinguishing between routine aspects of the job and special cases that require new approaches or special expertise. By assuming the role of specialist, a person uses technical abilities and exercises judgment in complex situations. By bringing the full extent of his personality resources and emotional understanding to the task at hand, he gives his work its unique personal characteristics.

A person in her 30s is no longer a beginner, and some of the grandiosity of the previous period begins to modulate as very real accomplishments occur. The achievement of mastery and the recognition by others of her unique contribution can lead a person to a distinctive sense of her own independent stature. Psychological separation from the parents of childhood is thus experienced as more definitive.

---

2. Membership in a union, guild, or professional organization becomes more central to work life during this period. An expanding network of colleagues supplants the more intense and personal workplace friendships of earlier adulthood.

During this period one must balance needs for recognition with a sense of integrity and self-guidance. The need for recognition can, in some cases, take on an addictive quality, leading to a stunting of growth in work life. At the same time, though, a concern with personal reputation is a cornerstone of work life during this period. As he increasingly moves into a public sphere, the individual must take into consideration how others see his values, skills, and accomplishments. Work is less and less a private affair, and a person in his 30s must take adequate care of how he is seen by others in order for his work life to develop.

The Age of Mastery typically coincides with pregnancy, childbirth, and child rearing. When work takes on the added significance of providing for children, it assumes new layers of psychological meaning. Work more fully becomes an expression of "generativity" (Erikson, 1950), a means by which one takes care of others. With parenthood, one may bring a new-found maturity and depth of commitment to her involvement in work. The experience of bonding with an infant or young child may facilitate a deeper sense of connectedness to others in the workplace. The intense feelings of love and hate that arise in child rearing may put the relationships of the workplace into greater perspective, as one gains increased poise in dealing with others at work.

Parenthood may become a means of creative self-expression that overshadows the rewards of work life. Deep reparative urges gain expression through parenthood in ways that they typically cannot in work life and lead, in some cases, to a decreased investment in work. Work may actually come to be resented during this period because it means giving up time with children and family. In other cases, though, parenthood may engender anxieties and conflicts that lead a person to throw himself into what feels like the safer, more structured, and impersonal world of work.

Working to safeguard and provide for a family may require giving up "dreams of glory" in work life. For some, this gives a new-found reality and sense of rootedness to their work life. Others cannot accept this development, feel that they have betrayed their dreams, and resent the compromises they find themselves making. It is not uncommon for men in particular to ruminate about what they imagine they might have been if they had not had to settle down and raise a family.

Parenthood requires the setting of complex boundaries between self and partner, work life and personal life, time for others and time for oneself. The Age of Mastery refers, then, not only to the world of work, but also to mastery of the conflicting time and emotional demands of work life, personal life, and family life. The risk increases during this period of role stress, flight from responsibilities, increased marital conflict, and rigid-ification of the personality. The difficulty in balancing work and family has become more acute as women have entered the full-time workforce in unprecedented numbers over the past 25 years. Achieving a sense of bal-ance, for both men and women, is essential to personality integration and growth in adulthood. Yet it seems as elusive as it is important. The prob-lem of work—family balance, which is of such widespread concern in our culture now, is discussed in more detail in chapter 9.

MIDLIFE

The Midlife Transition

Midlife has been seen by some as beginning in the mid-30s (Jaques, 1965) and by others as beginning in the early 40s (Levinson et al., 1978). Consensus exists among adult developmentalists, though, that there is a transitional period of several years sometime between 35 and 45 that may be so tumultuous as to constitute a "midlife crisis." This transition period has critical importance for subsequent psychological development in gen-eral and for work life in particular.

In his classic article "Death and the Midlife Crisis" Elliott Jaques (1965) identified the key psychological tasks associated with the transi-tion to middle age. At the midpoint of life, perhaps precipitated by phys-iological changes such as diminished libido, one is faced with the reality of one's own eventual death. This confrontation with one's mortality necessitates the reworking of the infantile depressive position, and in this the balance between love and hatred in the personality is decisive. An appropriate sense of grief and resignation when one is faced with the inevitability of death can lead to growth and the enrichment of personality described by Jaques as follows:

> The gain is in the deepening of awareness, understanding, and self-realization. Genuine values can be cultivated—of wisdom, fortitude, and courage, deeper capacity for love and affection and human insight, and hopefulness and enjoyment—qualities whose genuineness stems from inte-gration based upon the more immediate and self-conscious awareness and acceptance not only of one's own shortcomings but of one's destructive impulses, and from the greater capacity for sublimation which accompanies true resignation and detachment [p. 327].

Several authors have elaborated on Jaques's core theme. Modell (1989) observed that middle age is characterized by a mourning of lost illusions and a coming to terms with the limitations of the self, loved ones, and reality. Auchincloss and Michels (1989) noted that ambitions and ideals, formed under the influence of childhood fantasy must be updated in the face of the new, overriding realties of middle age. Levinson et al. (1978) focused on the process of "de-illusionment" during the midlife transition, that requires the man "to begin to grieve and accept the symbolic death of the youthful hero within himself" (p. 215). Vaillant (1993) has remarked on the diminished social anxiety and increased freedom from what others think that can accompany this de-illusionment.

A central component of the midlife transition is the reappraisal of one's work life. The heightened awareness of one's mortality typically leads to reflection on one's involvement in work, especially one's goals and guiding ideals. There is a potential at this time for fundamental change in the relationship to work and further individuation of the personality through work life. A more nuanced understanding of success and failure, a recasting of ideals related to work life, and a reevaluation of the role of work in one's life may occur during this period.

The meaning and value of work-related success is often not questioned until the midlife transition. An increased sense of the finiteness of one's life often illuminates the reality of one's successes and failures up to this point. An acceptance of specific failures and a more forgiving attitude toward failure in general may lead to a strengthening of the personality. A deeper appreciation of one's unique talents and skills as well as one's limitations may lead to a refinement or even a major change in vocational goals. Success may be redefined in less conventional and more personal terms with a view to what will ultimately be one's legacy.

The midlife transition signals a qualitative change in the "personal dream" (Levinson et al. 1978) and is often accompanied by a major recasting of work-related ideals. Driving ambition and the dreams of glory that animated the work life of the young adult begin to recede during the midlife transition. The middle-aged adult is no longer a "dreamer," and if he is it is usually a cause for concern. As the "heroic illusion" (Axelrod, 1997) of early adulthood fades, a new sense of purpose needs to be found that will animate work life through middle adulthood. Conventional ideas of success may give way to more personal goals, as the person becomes better able to articulate what she stands for in the world of work, what she can contribute, and what rewards she hopes to obtain.

The midlife transition may bring about a reshaping of work-related ideals. Neugarten (1968) noted the growth of "interiority" during middle age, with the pleasures of being, experiencing, and understanding taking precedence over the excitement of striving and reaching. Work-related ideals may center more on understanding, insight, and affiliation. Work may be entered into with a new spirit of generosity and a tolerance for imperfection. The interpersonal dimension of the job may assume new importance, especially for those who have devoted themselves to achieving technical expertise. For some, an inner restructuring of ideals dovetails with the demands of the workplace requiring the person to move beyond technical skill to learn how to manage more effectively and lead others. Even under optimal conditions, this shift from the technical to the more interpersonal may pose a difficult challenge, as the "rough edges" of one's relationships are brought into awareness and need to be addressed.

The personality restructuring associated with the midlife transition brings about a deeper, more nuanced time perspective. A person's relationship to his field of endeavor may change as he achieves a new appreciation of where the field has been and where it is going. Increased attunement to the flow of generations may lead the middle-aged person to seek out opportunities to mentor younger workers. True generative leadership, based less on force and more on understanding, influence, and strategic vision, may now become possible.

In some cases, the disequilibrium of the midlife transition may lead to a deemphasis on work life, with a shifting of interest and energy to non-work-related pursuits. A new understanding of the price paid for success may lead to a heightened sense that work should not be an end in itself. Family life, other relationships, or long suppressed interests or hobbies may be pursued "before it is too late." Levinson et al. (1978) have suggested that a deemphasis on work life is particularly adaptive for those without clear prospects for continuing advancement. Perhaps single-minded devotion to work life at middle age makes less and less sense for those who don't feel essential to the success of an enterprise or organization. But we are all familiar with cases of those at the top of the pyramid who feel an increased responsiveness to inner promptings and make work less of a priority in their lives.

Underlying shifts in gender identity at midlife may play a part in reshaping one's relationship to work. As I have noted elsewhere (Axelrod, 1997), the ego ideal typically becomes less sharply gendered at midlife. There is a tendency for men to incorporate nurturant and affilliative tendencies previously disavowed as feminine. This shift may lead to a stronger interpersonal focus at work, increased interest in mentoring and generative leadership, or to a deemphasis on work life itself. Women, in contrast, may become more aware of and less conflicted about their aggression (Neugarten, 1968), especially as it pertains to work life. As the period of childbirth and raising young children wanes, middle-aged women may feel a surge of energy and excitement about their work lives. Freed of some of the wrenching work–family conflicts, women during this period may enthusiastically seek advancement and start new ventures.

Midlife—Dominance and Succession

The middle-aged are the dominant generation in society, its natural leaders in political, professional, and intellectual life. They are the senior members of an organization or vocation and are entrusted with its overall health and well-being. It is they who typically carry the enterprise in a time of crisis and who define its unique character for a particular era. With their wealth of experience, the middle-aged are typically the ones who must resolve the difficult questions of ethics and values for the organization or vocation.

Most middle-aged persons must define their relationship to leadership in a way that makes sense for them. Leadership comes in many different shapes and forms. Most commonly, a sense of leadership derives from having direct supervisory responsibility for the work of others. But there are other, more informal but equally valid ways that one achieves a sense of leadership. For example, a sense of leadership may be achieved by the person on the shop floor who is looked to for his wisdom, problem-solving ability, and sense of perspective on day-to-day difficulties. Of course, for some, a sense of leadership is achieved outside the realm of work life entirely, for example, by coaching youngsters in team sports, leading volunteer activities, and the like.

What I, following Erikson (1950), would call "generative leadership" has several key components. From her unique vantage point on the sequence of generations, a middle-aged person can express concern for the growth of the younger and less experienced members of the workforce. She can teach them what they need to know about where the enterprise has been. Generative leadership is also based on a capacity for strategic thinking, an ability to take a long view of an organization or vocation, which is essential for its meaningful growth. It also requires an understanding of the enterprise as a whole and its interlocking relationships with other components of the field and the culture at large. The exercise of generative leadership is based on some clarity about human motivation and a demonstrated acceptance of one's own power and responsibility.

Generative leadership is characterized by a sense of having "been there" without being jaded and cynical about the future. While the middle-aged person knows he knows a lot, he is aware that he doesn't know everything. His understanding of the tradition of an enterprise and his wealth of experience do not foreclose the possibility of innovative change and doing things differently. Indeed, this is one of the hallmarks of generative leadership—an understanding that change is necessary and may come from sources other than oneself.

From a developmental perspective, there are two major ways in which work life can go awry during middle age: stagnation and destructive leadership. Erikson's epigenetic scheme postulated the duality of generativity versus stagnation during midlife. The inability to invest in the growth and development of succeeding generations leads to a depletion of inner resources, rigidification of the personality, and, sometimes, an outbreak of symptoms. Stagnation in work life is evident when a person, despairing of the capacity to innovate, works mostly by rote, going through the motions of methods and techniques that were previously successful. Ideals and goals are clung to even as they become increasingly unrealistic and lead to bitterness and cynicism. Depressive self-absorption can become evident in a devaluing of one's own and others' accomplishments, opposition to any change, and increasing alienation from the lifeblood of the organization and the vocation. Stagnation frequently manifests itself in psychosomatic disorders that can severely compromise work life. The high incidence of questionable disability claims during this period is indicative of the widespread experience of stagnation, of giving up and resentfully wanting to be taken care of.

The failure to achieve generative leadership is one of the costliest and most common problems in organizational life today. While cases abound of people in high positions whose leadership is characterized by the stagnation and emptiness I have described, I also want to emphasize the heavy costs exacted by "destructive leadership." Destructive leadership is motivated by outright envy of the next generations, of those who are being led. The malignant grandiosity of this type of leader grows in direct proportion to the loss of an inner sense of vitality. The use of force and coercion, the need to triumph at all costs, and the pleasure taken in destroying the careers of others are attempts to shore up a self that is fragmenting in the face of decline and death. The destructive leader focuses on the immediacy of the present rather than the future, his own self aggrandizement

rather than the well-being of the enterprise as a whole, the external trap-
pings of power and position rather than the inner transformation that is
so critical to generative leadership.

The later middle years are, according to Erikson (1950), characterized
by the achievement of ego integrity. To apply Erikson's description of ego
integrity to work life, this means that a person accepts her career as the
most authentic expression of the self. Ego integrity encompasses an appreciation of a person's unique contribution to her field of endeavor and a
sense of having made a difference in the course of her career. It also
implies an experience of completeness, and a capacity to face retirement
without dread and despair.

A person who achieves a sense of integrity in his work life feels not only
that he has accomplished something, but also that he can defend his decisions, accomplishments, and values against the trivial, ephemeral, or corrupt. A strong sense of what he has stood for, of his ideals and ambitions
tempered by reality, can be communicated to others. And while he takes
pride in his own contribution, he is aware that it is based on his unique
synthesis of ambition, ideals, and talents and that there could have been
and will be other ways to "get the job done." Under optimal conditions,
then, the person, no matter how humble his circumstances, achieves a
sense of his own legacy with regard to his work life. The legacy itself can
serve a selfobject function (Kohut, 1977) that strengthens him sufficiently
to negotiate succession and retirement.

The need to plan for succession during late midlife can stir up internal
conflict that is then externalized with adverse consequences. Even someone who has been able to mentor younger workers may balk at handing
over the reins and achieving closure on her work life. If retirement is experienced as a narcissistic injury, the transition to new leadership may be sab-
otaged. The person may unconsciously try to bind the job or organization
ever more tightly to her identity, thereby delegitimating her successors and
creating confusion around her.

Attitudes toward aging in the organization and the culture at large can
influence the experience of succession and retirement in late midlife. The
increasing skew toward youth in organizational life means fewer opportunities for those in later midlife. The firing and otherwise marginalizing
of people in their 50s and 60s mean that movement toward retirement can
become dominated by anger, resentment, and confusion. Currently, there
are grounds for concern that the vast majority of those in late middle age
will feel that they are becoming obsolete and are being forced out of the
organization. Although some may be resilient enough to cope with these

circumstances by starting new careers as consultants or entrepreneurs, doing so requires a capacity for risk taking and working on one's own that is difficult for many. A person facing succession and retirement needs to feel that she has been valued for her unique perspective as a senior member of the enterprise. If, as a society, we are becoming less able to provide this kind of validation, then the very real successes of our economy threaten to ring hollow.

3

The Concept of
Work Disturbance

Psychoanalytic treatment requires the clinician's day-to-day attention to her patient's work-related problems. Patients spend more time at work than in any other single activity, so it is only to be expected that work would be a major focus of any treatment. And while in our actual work with patients we *do* attend to many work-related issues, we do so, I believe, in only a piecemeal fashion. We are too quick to shift the focus from the content of work life to early development or the transference, thereby subtly neglecting the full richness of our patients' work lives. Because we typically do not develop a systematic, psychodynamic understanding of work-related problems as a discrete area of focus, we lose opportunities to help our patients make progress in an area of great concern to them.

Typically, our thinking about our patients' work difficulties is global, limited to support for career change and advancement and to the resolution of specific interpersonal problems in the workplace. The presenting complaints of many of our patients include some form of career dissatisfaction, and we try to help them better define what they want and achieve it. We support changes in career, hoping or assuming that change will be a move toward more fulfilling and personally meaningful work. We may even identify conflicts related to competition and success as part of helping patients advance in their careers. In actual sessions, we get a sense of our patients' relationships in the workplace and help our patients think about them in transferential terms.

I believe, however, that we don't frequently enough grasp the pattern over time of our patients' work difficulties, and their roots in the uncon-

35

scious. Rarely do we think systematically about their actual task functioning—the capacities to employ reality testing, focal concentration, judgment, time perspective, impulse control. Nor do we think enough about our patients' relationship to work qua work: how success and failure as well as work and play are represented; how important needs are gratified or not; how relevant interests were developed in the crucible of the family; how work-related values and ideals were formed and maintained; how patterns of drive, defense, and unconscious fantasy color work life.

I believe that the concept of work disturbance can help us understand some of the most common patternings of our patients' work-related problems and can guide our interventions. The concept of work disturbance encompasses typical modes of task functioning, interpersonal relationships, and core psychodynamic factors. It is an integrative concept that is meant to address a fundamental disconnection between workplace observation and counseling, on one hand, and psychoanalytic treatment, on the other. The former focuses on maladaptive patterns of interpersonal relationships and task performance that are addressed through behavioral interventions. Psychoanalytic treatment usually focuses on developmental factors and unconscious dynamics without adequate reference to actual workplace behavior. Using the "work disturbance" concept, which links both domains of functioning, can, I believe, greatly enhance the power of a clinician's interventions.

The description of some of the most common forms of work disturbance in chapters 4 through 6 is an attempt to order the wide range of work-related problems commonly encountered in clinical practice. These include work inhibition, work compulsion (or workaholism), work diffusion, and disillusionment and disability. To this point, there have been few efforts[1] to describe systematically the range of work problems encountered in clinical practice, although some useful accounts have been offered of specific forms of work difficulty and their treatment (Freud, 1916; Ovesey, 1962; Tartakoff, 1966; Fast, 1975; Kramer, 1977; Satow, 1988; Stark, 1989).

The concept of work disturbance presumes that work is represented in relatively enduring ways that can be inferred from work-related behavior and associations to that behavior in clinical interviews. This is not to say that the specifics of a particular job are not important or that a person will not feel and behave differently in a different setting. Rather, work disturbance applies in cases where personality functioning vis-à-vis work is rel-

---

1. The work of Kets de Vries (1978) is an exception and is frequently noted in this book.

atively rigid so that the characteristic relationship to work tends to repeat itself across specific settings. In these cases, intervention is most effective when geared both to the specifics of a particular job and to the more general pattern that has come to characterize the patient's work life.

Work disturbance is a more encompassing phenomenon than the specific workplace transferences frequently addressed in psychoanalytic treatment. Work disturbance entails a disruption of a person's *overall* relationship to work life. At different times, specific workplace transferences, *as components of a work disturbance*, become a focus of intervention. Indeed, the interpretation of these transferences is one of the most potent ways of ameliorating a work disturbance. The treatment of a work disturbance, however, requires the clinician to intervene more broadly in the patient's relationship to work.

In the most general sense, all forms of work disturbance entail some impairment in the capacity for satisfaction and pleasure in work life. While there is usually some interference with productivity, the presence of a work disturbance does not entirely preclude some real success in work life. Rather, a work disturbance revolves around the fact that, *as the individual experiences it,* work plays a deeply problematic role in his life. His work life is a source of frustration or dissatisfaction to him, in some cases because he feels it has assumed excessive importance and the drive for success has taken him over.

Work disturbance typically entails the substitution of some form of fantasized or neurotic satisfaction for the real satisfactions work life can bring. The satisfactions encapsulated by a work disturbance may include revenge through failure, omnipotent control over others, dreams of glory that have no chance for actual completion, and many others.

A work disturbance consists of a patterning of the self in relation to work life that is expressed in a typical configuration of drive, defense, affect, and interpersonal relationships. In general, a work disturbance entails some impairments in reality appraisal, the capacity to sustain focal concentration on a task, and the ability to obtain pleasure from the achievement of goals. Self-esteem is typically impaired or poorly regulated, and negative affects, especially fear, anger, shame, disappointment, and anxiety tend to dominate work life. Maladaptive patterns of workplace relationships, including hostility or excessive compliance toward those in authority, exploitation of subordinates, withdrawal from and mistrust of coworkers, and the like, become prominent and are repetitively enacted.

The relationship between work-related problems and psychopathology is illustrated in Figure 1. The vertically shaded area, A, represents individuals with significant psychopathology who do not have a work disturbance. These include two major groups. Those in group A1 are at their best in the workplace. Their psychopathology has less impact on their work than on any other domain of functioning. Indeed, this is a group that may use work to "hold themselves together." Those in group A2 import more of their pathology into the workplace. It is not that their psychopathology is elicited by working in particular; rather, their overall symptomatology compromises their ability to function in the workplace. For individuals in both areas A1 and A2 work itself does not have an unusually strong negative valence.

The horizontally shaded area, B, describes those individuals who present work-related problems in the relative absence of psychopathology. This population consists of three main groups—those experiencing episodes of work-related stress, those seeking help for career development, and those participating in some form of organizational intervention. In all three cases, the workplace is strongly determinative and, although personality style and psychopathology may be important, they are not a focus of intervention.

Although work-related stress may become a focus for clinical intervention, it is distinct from a work disturbance per se. Workplace stress reactions occur when the perceived environmental demand exceeds a person's coping abilities, as in cases of excessive work load or work pace or poorly defined work roles. The focus of intervention in these cases is the work environment itself. The individual must act to redefine his relationship to the demands of the work environment, either within the job or by

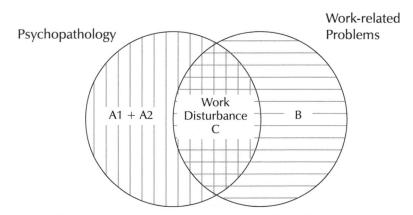

Figure 1. The Relationship Between Work-related Problems and Psychopathology

changing jobs. In some cases, once work-related stress is addressed, an underlying work disturbance may emerge and require treatment.

Area B includes problems that are rooted in the work group itself and are addressed in that context. Menzies (1975), Hirschhorn (1988), and others have shown how disturbances in group process interfere with task performance and goal attainment in the workplace. Psychoanalytically oriented organizational consultants see the *group* as the patient; they assume that workplace difficulties derive not from individual work disturbances but from defenses employed by the group to cope with change and anxiety-provoking tasks. Effective organizational consultation leads to growth in the individual as well as to the team's work functioning. This form of intervention, however, presumes a relative absence of individual work disturbance, and the effectiveness of the intervention may be limited by its presence.

The largest group within area B are individuals engaged in some form of career intervention. Included in this group are those who seek guidance and counseling in changing careers. It also includes individuals functioning quite well at work who want to enhance their growth and development through a focus on work life. Workplace coaching interventions are geared toward this group; although, as coaching proceeds, either a work disturbance or gross psychopathology may emerge, requiring therapeutic intervention. This group also includes patients in psychotherapy for whom career development becomes a major focus of intervention, as is described in more detail in chapter 8.

The cross-hatched area, C, describes individuals with a form of work disturbance. These are patients with both significant psychopathology *and* particular difficulties in work life. Work life has a high degree of salience and is a primary arena in which these individuals' personality difficulties are played out. The special demand characteristics of work life affect how the personality disturbance is manifested; the interplay between the key dimensions of work life and the central dynamics of the personality disorder defines the types of work disturbance.

The relationship between work disturbance and psychiatric diagnosis is a complex one. There is no one-to-one correspondence between the two. As noted with regard to area A, some rather impaired people function relatively well at work. A psychiatric diagnosis suggests how the personality is organized globally but does not explain the degree of impact on work functioning. And, although diagnostic categories tend to cluster around specific forms of work disturbance, it is more likely that a specific work disturbance will be linked to certain personality *traits* (e.g., obsessive-compulsive, narcissistic, borderline) than to a psychiatric diagnosis per se. The important point is that the work disturbance concept adds an important dimension to our understanding of a patient beyond her diagnosis. A description of a patient's work disturbance provides a richer, more unified picture of the individual's work life than does any single diagnosis. It encompasses a description of personality traits, core psychodynamic and developmental issues, and indications for intervention focused on work functioning.

Broad descriptors of the level of personality functioning, such as neurotic versus borderline or oedipal versus preoedipal, are used in formulating the most common forms of work disturbance. For example, work inhibition is considered primarily an oedipal-level phenomenon, work diffusion primarily a preoedipal phenomenon. I believe that these concepts are useful in understanding work disturbance because they carry with them strong developmental implications. Even so, we are now much more sophisticated about the coexistence of preoedipal and oedipal trends within the same personality, so that a particular form of work disturbance suggests only the *relative* prominence of the overall developmental level vis-à-vis work life.

4

Work Inhibition and Work Compulsion

Work inhibition is the form of work disturbance most commonly encountered in clinical practice. In the workplace it is characterized by restricted productivity and sometimes by the derailment of previously good performance. In the consulting room it is distinguished by fear of success as well as conflicts over aggression and competition.

The work-inhibited person has generally intact, though often obsessional, thinking. He is industrious and perfectionistic, though often indecisive and prone to procrastination. He has an excessive fear of making mistakes and exaggerates the adverse effects of his errors. He is usually not as productive as he would like to think he is, a fact that is apparent to coworkers and supervisors and often to his therapist as well. The work-inhibited person is usually not in doubt about his field of endeavor and may display an unwavering commitment to his particular career. He approaches the workplace in terms of right and wrong, duty and obligation, what should and shouldn't be done. He believes that if he works hard he *should* achieve success and may seem to others to have a sense of entitlement.

In cases of work inhibition, basic ego functions are intact *within the restricted range of the individual's work-related activity*. However, higher order ego functions such as strategic thinking and vision are not well developed. The work-inhibited person seeks security and feels safe with rules and standard procedures, even though she may long for creative self-expression. She is more comfortable working hard at defined tasks given to her than in generating the work herself, which often involves self-promotion, selling, and persuading. She is risk averse and finds change anxiety provoking. This type of person might have felt more comfortable in traditional, hierarchical organizations, but she is less suited to today's rapidly changing workplace.

Patients with work inhibition often assume a dry, businesslike, sometimes aloof manner in the workplace. Typically, task performance is emphasized at the expense of interpersonal functioning. Some may function quite well as long as they are working primarily in a technical capacity. They run into trouble, however, when they have to assume more managerial and leadership functions or when they have to take a more public posture that depends more on social contacts. Under these circumstances, when more give and take with other people is required, a lack of interpersonal fluency becomes evident.

Team functioning can be difficult for work-inhibited individuals because they are excessively devoted to the way things *should* be in the workplace and what people *should* do. Being so bound to proscriptive behavior, they may actually be quite naive when it comes to the realities of power and influence. They mistrust the fluidity of team dynamics and often express a preference for doing things themselves. Under stress in working with other people they may become stubborn and argumentative, insisting on what they consider the correct or highly principled way of doing things, often derailing the functioning of the group. As subordinates, while they may appear dutiful and responsible, they are often covertly critical and resentful of authority. As bosses, they tend to be demanding and unforgiving, controlling and reluctant to delegate. They usually demonstrate little warmth and are not viewed with affection by their subordinates.

The interpersonal and task functioning of work-inhibited individuals provide fertile ground for counseling and coaching interventions. Such people may respond well to efforts to improve interpersonal and communication skills, and in some cases these interventions may help resolve underlying conflicts around aggression, competition, and success. The effectiveness of these more behavioral approaches, however, may be limited by core conflicts that can be addressed only in a treatment setting.

THE PSYCHODYNAMICS OF WORK INHIBITION

Work inhibition is the form of work disturbance most commonly seen clinically and consistently described in the psychoanalytic literature. Beginning with Freud (1916), psychoanalytic authors have linked work inhibition to neurotic conflicts associated with rivalry, aggression, and guilt (see Ovesey, 1962; Kets de Vries, 1978). These cases are best understood in terms of a harsh and punitive superego and the developmental factors that give rise to it. The superego concept links the surface of conscientious but rule-bound and moralistic workplace behavior with the depth of conflicts over success. These are oedipal-stage issues that are consistent with the obsessive–compulsive, passive–aggressive, and avoidant personality types that seem to cluster with this form of work disturbance.

"Those Wrecked by Success," described by Freud (1916) provides one model of work inhibition. Drawing on characters from the plays of Shakespeare and Ibsen, Freud described cases in which the achievement of a long-sought goal led to an outbreak of symptoms and a deterioration of functioning. He explained this seeming paradox in terms of an unconscious sense of guilt. The achievement of success is unconsciously equated with the gratification of forbidden sexual and aggressive impulses, thus setting in motion powerful self-punishing forces.

Both Ovesey (1962) and Kets de Vries (1978) described forms of work inhibition that they linked to problems with the aggressive drive. Ovesey believed that the fear of vocational success is a common phobic syndrome. He postulated that work inhibition has its origins in the early rivalries of a child with both parents and siblings. Where there are problems in the management of aggression in the family of origin (e.g., severe intimidation, hostile competitiveness, etc.) a symbolic equation is made between aggression and violence. Because of this association of aggression with violent destructiveness, all forms of assertiveness become inhibited. The unconscious desire to destroy more powerful rivals, which is a normal motivational dynamic in vocational success, becomes associated early on with enormous guilt and fear of retaliation. Instead of being directed outward, aggression becomes inner directed, leading to work paralysis. Thus, the individual, beset by inordinate guilt, withdraws from competition in order to protect himself from murderous retaliation.

In his discussion of a psychoanalytic case, Kramer (1977) explicitly linked his patient's work difficulties to oedipal guilt. Kramer suggested that, for this man, work was equated with the acquisition of the "omnipotent paternal phallus," with murderous wishes toward the father and therefore with unbearable guilt. Like most patients with a work inhibition, Kramer's patient developed a harsh, sadistic superego "based on the introjection of the mental representation of the father as a powerful, cruel, oppressive tyrant" (p. 377). Restricted activity, leaving projects fragmented and unfinished, became simultaneously a way of rebelling against the superego command for commitment and responsibility and a means of avoiding the castration anxiety that would accompany success.

Ovesey (1962) drew a useful distinction between those more passive, obsessional persons for whom the aggression is "inhibited at its source" and the more paranoid persons whose aggression is inhibited at the "executive end." The latter are overwhelmed with the wish for assertion and are terrified of losing control of it. Following Ovesey in this regard, I suggest that there are two distinct forms of work inhibition, both rooted in developmental problems with aggression as it is expressed in rivalry and competitiveness. "Success phobia," in which aggression is "inhibited at its source," is associated with a chronic personality disorder. Productivity is restricted, and success is elusive. Those with success phobia typically have a history of underachievement in school and at work. Those with a second kind of work inhibition—"those wrecked by success"—are characterized by an expansive personality, the achievement of some measure of success, but a subsequent outbreak of symptoms upon achievement of a goal. These people often have paranoid traits, and it is their anxious scanning of the environment for signs of their rivals' disapproval or retaliation that sets in motion their deterioration of functioning at the point of accomplishment.

In treating a work inhibition, the therapist must consistently attend to what the patient is *not* doing that prevents other people from being comfortable with her and thus keeps her at the periphery of the workplace. Often, the patient's aloofness stems from a hidden anger and contempt toward others for not doing things the right way or up to the proper standards. That is, the patient externalizes his own punitive superego in the workplace. Material related to the patient's excessive devotion to a "right way" of doing things, and criticalness of others in the workplace can become a focus of the patient's treatment. The therapist may confront the patient's anger about how the organization and the people in it do not live up to his expectations.

The therapist may at times want to make explicit to the work inhibited patient that a job consists of more than task and technique—communication and group process skills as well as an appreciation of different personality styles are equally important. If treatment is successful, the patient comes to view the workplace in more flexible terms and to enter more fully into the relationships that are necessary for getting things done.

The essential characteristics of a work inhibition are often repeated in the treatment itself. Not only are these patients given to intellectualization rather than experiencing, they tend to approach the treatment as a procedure that is devoid of the more personal aspects of the therapist–patient relationship. They tend to "follow the rules" of treatment and strive to be considered good patients. Therefore, change may come slowly. Exploration of resistances may reveal transference paradigms based on stubborn opposition and competitiveness with the therapist. Fear of the therapist's power and anxiety that assertiveness and disagreement with the therapist will have adverse consequences are also common.

Case Example: Geoff N

Geoff presented many of the characteristics of chronic work inhibition or success phobia when he entered psychotherapy in his late 30s. He complained of procrastination, an avoidance of routine written work and phone calls, and excessive drowsiness at work. This public-sector employee had failed to advance in his department and had put off looking for work that would enable him better to support his two young children. He seemed to get caught up in interoffice rivalries and resentment toward his supervisors and found it difficult to mobilize the necessary support for projects that were important to him. He felt best in anticipation of taking on "the powers that be" but often had difficulty putting into action his fantasies of cutting them to ribbons with his displays of fact and logic.

The younger of two sons, Geoff described himself as a shy, overweight child with a stutter. He remembered having been beaten and bullied mercilessly by his older brother and teased by his peers. He was neither understood nor protected by a distant, overworked father or an emotionally unstable mother.

As an adolescent, Geoff came to see that his command of facts and use of logic enabled him to do well in school and at times successfully to challenge his teachers. He had begun to transform the fear and humiliation of his childhood into a personal mythology of triumphing against overwhelming odds in his academic, and later professional, life. Over time, however, this personal mythology became more and more constricting. "Fighting the good fight" proved an inadequate means of channeling his rivalry and aggression; all too often he reexperienced the helplessness and frustration of childhood. By tying himself to a series of losing battles, he not only reexperienced the humiliation of defeat by a more powerful rival, but also was blocked from having an experience of adult power and authority.

Psychotherapy enabled Geoff to work through some of his anger toward both his parents and his brother. He was able to express his sadness over his father's increasing ill health and senility; at one point he cried because it was now too late to connect with his father on a deeper level. Although sessions remained dry and intellectualized, Geoff came to value more highly the expression of feelings to his therapist and to others in his life who might be receptive.

As for Geoff's work life, the balance began to shift away from aggressive fantasy toward more realistic action. Some lessening of his rigid and punitive superego led to a heightened sense of pleasure and effectiveness in interpersonal relationships in the workplace. He felt a greater closeness to some of his colleagues. At the same time, he was able to accept that much of what he had hoped to get from the heads of his department would not be forthcoming, largely because of the limitations of their own personalities and positions. In short, he became able to see the workplace more for what it in fact was than for what it should have been. When the political tide turned even more dramatically against his department, Geoff was finally able to "read the handwriting on the wall" and to make a long overdue change. He found another job in the public interest with better pay and more potential for effectiveness.

Case Example: Charles G

Charles started treatment at age 35 for symptoms of depression. He had recently ended yet another relationship and felt stuck vocationally.

After years of working at unskilled jobs, Charles had learned computer programming and achieved a stable position. However, he saw his position as a nontechnical one and thus of low status. He longed for, but did not have the confidence to apply for, a more technical position.

Although responsible and task oriented, he was highly risk averse. He feared speaking in meetings and initiating contacts with new clients. Charles complained of the arbitrariness of the company's director and the ineptitude of his immediate supervisor; he had a strong sense of how the company should be run and how its employees should be treated. Yet he was paralyzed in his interactions with superiors by a combination of rage and fear. His feelings of humiliation in such situations soon became a major concern in Charles's treatment.

Charles had been raised in a lower middle-class family, the older of two children. His mother had grown up in a succession of orphanages and foster homes. His father had been beaten by his own father but, in spite of problems with drinking and fighting, had managed to complete high school and get a steady job. Charles's younger brother had had a troubled adolescence and died of a drug overdose in his early 20s.

Charles had feared his parents, who both had problems controlling their temper. He resented his mother for being overprotective and his father for being distant and uninvolved. As a child, he felt weak and estranged from other children. Although he had good aptitude, he did not particularly like school and was soon labeled an underachiever. After high school he enrolled in college but soon dropped out, beginning a pattern that would continue through his 20s. He moved to the city, was fascinated by the world of artists and intellectuals, and joined the "counterculture." He was struggling to leave behind the provincial world he had grown up in, but he still felt like a child in the world of adults when he started treatment.

Charles's unconscious equation of aggression with violent destructiveness and his proneness to shame and guilt were characteristic of success phobia. He had grown up in a family where the latent threat of violence had sometimes given way to cruel parental behavior. He was afraid of his distant, authoritarian father and was erotically tied to his mother. Charles was guilt ridden over his oedipal strivings; a series of medical problems in childhood and adolescence were unconsciously equated with castration. He was also left with an enormous burden of guilt over his rivalry with his brother, who later destroyed himself.

In treatment, Charles was overly polite and deferential. He tried to figure out the "rules" of therapy and gain the therapist's approval by complying with them. Eventually, his resentment of these strictures began to surface in the therapy. His experience of the therapist as a distant, arbitrary figure began to resemble his experiences with his parents and bosses. As he began to work through some of the issues related to authority and his own aggression, Charles became more comfortable with coworkers and more accomplished at work. His longing for a closer relationship with the therapist ushered in a period of analysis that focused on underlying perverse trends in the personality. As the analysis moved deeper, the success phobia gave way to a different form of work disturbance, one coinciding with the preoedipal issues that were emerging in the transference, dreams, and fantasies. (This phase of his work life is described when we return to the case of Charles in chapter 7.)

WORK COMPULSION

Although work inhibition and its treatment have been described in some detail in the psychoanalytic literature, "work compulsion" has not, although it is probably more characteristic of contemporary culture than any other form of work disturbance. Work compulsion, a term I use interchangeably with workaholism, presents as an addiction to work, a preference for working over any other activity. Because the compulsion to work is so adaptive in a culture that is preoccupied with productivity, it is often not a focus of treatment. The workaholic is often richly rewarded for his devotion to work life.

Workaholism is characterized by an *inner* compulsion to overwork. Being in a very demanding job does not per se define a work compulsion, although workaholics do tend to gravitate toward such jobs. The key to workaholism is the person's feeling that she has no choice but to work long hours, to be intensely absorbed in one project after another. Trying to show a workaholic that she can turn down projects and work less is often futile, leading only to a barrage of rationalizations about the importance of the work, the fact that the job requires long hours, and so on. The workaholic lives to work, will often work to the point of exhaustion, and may be perceived by others as killing herself by overworking. And whereas a better integrated person may get real pleasure from her accomplishments, the workaholic frequently does not. When the defenses are less effective, work activity is accompanied by anxiety, feelings of inadequacy, and feelings of being trapped.

In the workplace, the workaholic typically seeks control, power, and domination. Problems in using work as a means of channeling the aggressive drive (see chapter 1) are an important part of the workaholic's difficulties. He tends to be aggressive and competitive, seeing others as obstacles to achieving his goals. He may define his own strength in terms of others' weaknesses and may try to lead by force and intimidation.

A lack of balance between work life and personal life is a hallmark of the compulsion to work. The workaholic has marked difficulty with the lack of structure and goal directedness of home life and may try to avoid time at home. She prefers the concrete predictability of outer reality to the complexity and intangibility of emotional life. Her striving to get results takes her only so far in intimate relationships, often to her genuine surprise. As sophisticated and accomplished as she may be in work life, the workaholic is often extremely simple minded or downright clueless in her relationship life. It is usually the workaholic's partner who identifies the problem—in spite of all indications to the contrary, the workaholic steadfastly maintains that everything is fine in the relationship.

The phenomenon of workaholism has received practically no attention in the psychoanalytic literature. Only Kets de Vries (1978) has described the dynamics of workaholism. He linked the workaholic's incessant, frantic work activity to an overinvestment in the "grandiose self." A work life that centers on power and omnipotence serves to counteract the workaholic's experiences of helplessness and fragmentation. Kets de Vries emphasized the fragile nature of the work adjustment in these cases—any interference with the grandiose fantasies can lead to apathy, passivity, and stress reactions.

I agree with Kets de Vries that the compulsion to work is often seen in the context of significant narcissistic pathology. Grandiosity and attempts at control and domination in the workplace are layered over deeply rooted feelings of emptiness, helplessness, and fragmentation. Compulsive work activity suggests a primary problem in self-regulation, and problems with aggression are best seen as efforts to shore up a vulnerable self. The weakness of the self-structures is evident in a proneness to stress reactions and psychosomatic disorders of various forms.

In my experience, the early lives of workaholics are often characterized by experiences of loss, trauma, or deprivation within the nuclear family. Feelings of shame about one's background (including minority status and poverty) often underlie the grandiose strivings and excessive needs for control that characterize work life.

The workaholic is often highly resistant to treatment. He is threatened by the lack of structure and specified procedures in the psychotherapeutic situation and feels uncomfortable with the emphasis on feelings. Typically resorting to externalization and projection, he focuses on the weaknesses and inadequacies of those around him, including the therapist. Devaluing of the treatment process is common, along with frequent complaints of a lack of results. Lateness and missed sessions, ostensibly due to a demanding work schedule, may represent efforts to wrest control of and even defeat the treatment. The therapist may find himself maneuvered into accommodating the patient's hectic schedule, granting requests for practical advice, and focusing too much on work-related problems, all the while wondering if he has anything of real value to offer the patient.

Case Example: Anne Z

Anne Z, a 30-year-old associate at a large law firm, came to treatment with complaints of job-related stress. She was exhausted by overworking but at the same time felt inadequate on the job and was devastated by any criticism. She had temper outbursts at subordinates in the workplace and with her husband at home.

Anne had been recruited to her firm by one of her law school professors. This older man had been kind and supportive, but when he left the firm Anne felt adrift in a sea of sharks. As an associate, she lived in constant fear of the partners' criticism of her written work and technical abilities. Her feelings of inadequacy were projected onto her subordinates, whom she criticized as stupid, lazy, and out to cause problems for her. Thus, she was able to maintain some equilibrium, albeit an uneasy one, between fear and anger, feelings of inadequacy and superiority.

Anne was ambitious and perfectionistic. She worked long hours, sometimes driving herself to the point of exhaustion and illness. She was extremely task focused, was suspicious of coworkers, and had little use for socializing in the workplace. Anne viewed the workplace as a hierarchy and was very attuned to the nuances of status. Raised in a traditional culture but not a native English speaker, she was very aware of who had good manners, spoke well, and, most important, wrote fluently.

Anne had great difficulty relaxing both at work and in her personal life. She seemed most comfortable working and getting things done. She conveyed little interest in leisure time pursuits and in therapy spoke very little about her relationships outside work. She was driven to achieve, and the affectional currents of her friendships and even her marital relationship were barely mentioned in the treatment.

Anne had been born and raised in a foreign country. She was an only child and recalled a special relationship with her father, who died suddenly of unknown causes when she was six. Soon thereafter her mother went to work overseas, leaving her in the care of her godmother. She remembered the godmother as exceptionally strict and cold, beating Anne for any sign of laziness in school or at home. She had lived in fear of her godmother, much as she now lived in fear of the senior partners she worked for. Anne saw her mother only during annual vacations until they immigrated to the United States when Anne was an early adolescent.

Anne was deeply ashamed of not having a father and of having grown up in poverty. As a schoolgirl she made up stories to hide the loss of her father and the absence of her mother. Anne felt lonely and rejected by her peers and was the poor relation in her extended family. She devoted herself to being the best student in the class and soothed herself with thoughts of being more intelligent and more beautiful than the other girls.

As an adolescent and college student in New York, Anne was hard working, prim and proper, and rather aloof. She was popular in college and had many dates but did not get particularly close to anybody. In part-time and later full-time jobs, she kept her distance. Others, especially girls, saw her as a snob.

After less than a year of therapy, Anne, hoping to reduce her continuing symptoms of stress, took an extended, temporary assignment at a different branch of her firm. This practice was more academic, and she was impressed by the intellectual, sophisticated managing partner who now became her new mentor. She enjoyed working for him, and her symptoms of stress began to lessen.

When the temporary assignment ended, however, and Anne became a permanent employee on a partnership track, the pressure again increased. Anne began to find her mentor self-interested, critical, and demanding. She was envious of the other associates, whom she felt were unfairly favored and would be promoted sooner than she would be. After a hiatus from her feelings of inadequacy, Anne again despaired of having the coveted technical skills that would earn her the kind of partnership offer that would confirm her self worth.

In therapy, Anne focused almost exclusively on her work life, as if the treatment were de facto a kind of job coaching. She spoke very little about her husband or any aspect of her intimate life, although it became evident that hers was far from the ideal marriage that she had initially described. Anne was able to work through some of her disappointment in the managing partner and learned to "live without him." She gained a better understanding of the sources of her anger and competitiveness and felt more in control of her behavior. She learned to get along better with coworkers, although she could still treat her subordinates as her critical, demanding godmother had treated her. In the course of treatment, Anne became more confident of her technical skills. She became less anxious, and her self-esteem became more stable. The turning point came when Anne took a risk in turning down a sales-oriented partnership and, in so doing, actively defined herself as a player on the technical side of the business. Eventually, Anne was recommended for a prestigious technical job in the government similar to one held by her mentor many years earlier.

Case Example: Mark C

Mark was 46 and recently married for the first time when his wife convinced him to enter treatment because of a marked decrease in sexual desire soon after their marriage. In the initial session, Mark seemed remarkably unconcerned about the problem. Although he felt bad about his wife's unhappiness and understood that something had to be done if they were to conceive a child, he claimed that he was otherwise quite satisfied with the relationship the way it was.

Mark had a long history of partial impotence and few serious relationships with women. He found the secretions and smells of sexual activity quite repugnant and was embarrassed for a woman to see *his* sexual excitement. Ejaculation represented a loss of control that he found mortifying.

In marked contrast, Mark described his career as a lawyer in terms of feeling powerful and in control. He had wanted to be a lawyer since childhood, when Clarence Darrow and Perry Mason had been his heroes. From junior high school through college and law school he had stood up to authority and pleaded his case. Mark eventually built a successful law practice and enjoyed the combat of litigation and the appreciation of his clients. He was proud of his success and presented himself as a carefully tailored, worldly attorney.

Mark declared proudly that for the better part of 20 years he had been "married to the law." He worked very long hours and often brought work home on the weekends. In his leisure time he liked to lie on the couch and watch TV; he seemed to enjoy little else. He enjoyed his wife's company on the weekends and vacations but, except for a few friends, had little interest in other people.

Mark had grown up an overprotected only child of middle-class parents. His mother had a history of disappointments and losses, a probable postpartum depression following his birth, and subsequent depressive symptoms. She cared for him efficiently but without much touching or physical comforting. His father showed more warmth but was eccentric, cranky, and bossy. Mark was toilet trained early and was described as a very neat and clean child. He was also rather solitary, playing for hours on end with his toy soldiers. He had found it extremely difficult, even well into adulthood, to break away from anxious, intrusive parents, who, he felt, lived vicariously through his accomplishments.

Mark found it very difficult to be a patient in psychotherapy. The ambiguity and open-endedness of psychotherapy were problematic for him, given his externalized, goal-directed view of the world. He requested instructions and directions from the therapist on a regular basis and mentioned "How to . . ." manuals and inspirational books as models of effective intervention. He seemed more interested in discussions of how therapy works than in actual psychotherapeutic exploration. Although he could get to court for a 9 AM case, he was never on time for his morning therapy sessions. The idea of disrupting his work schedule for makeup or additional sessions panicked him and led to combative interactions with the therapist.

Mark had difficulty describing either his feelings or his interactions with others. He was most aware of feeling panicked in situations where he was threatened with a loss of control. He recounted some dreams of fragmentation and fleeting daydreams of falling into a chasm and disappearing. Mark's descriptions of other people were impoverished. He described his wife as being in a cocoon with him; only occasionally did he experience her as a truly separate person. When she tried to explain to him that she wanted not only to become pregnant but to have a satisfying sexual relationship with him, Mark seemed baffled and frightened.

Mark did acknowledge that his life was not in balance. He looked to the therapist to reinforce his spending less time working and more unstructured time with his wife. He was able to understand that his work life had developed at the expense of other aspects of life that he found puzzling, frightening, and beyond his control. However, Mark remained deeply suspicious of the therapist. When relatively modest improvements in the marital relationship decreased his wife's pressure on him, his motivation for treatment lessened even further. He provoked a confrontation with the therapist and terminated treatment abruptly.

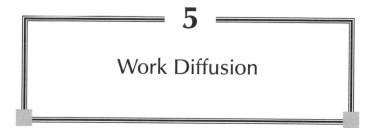

5

Work Diffusion

A lack of satisfaction in work is endemic to our time and is common to both normal work life and all forms of work disturbance. Chronic dissatisfaction with one's work life is, however, central to what I call "work diffusion." This form of work disturbance is characterized by an experienced lack of fit between the self and the work role that comes to preoccupy the patient. She feels unable to integrate different facets of the self—whether talents, values, or goals—with the actualities of work life. She feels frustrated by her inability to express who she is in her work life and typically feels trapped in the wrong job, career, or organization. Even if successful, she feels as though she is acting a part, and longs to express her true self. This is the kind of person who may ruminate for years about changing careers but is unable to take any realistic action to do so. Alternatives tend to be vaguely defined; they are more dreamed about than thought about.[1]

Work diffusion can be conceptualized in self-psychological terms as a failure of self-cohesion in the realm of work life. Work role identity is at issue for these people, as they actively struggle with such questions as "Who am I?" "What am I good at?" "What do I really want to do?" While such concerns, if transient, are not uncommon, they are suggestive of a work disturbance if they become an enduring preoccupation and source of frustration.

---

1. These people frequently find their way to career counselors but, owing to their severe character pathology, can have great difficulty making use of this focused and time-limited intervention. They are often best referred either for concomitant psychotherapy or to a clinically trained career counselor.

Confusion about ambition and ideals is a hallmark of work diffusion. These are people who may either lack a certain drive for working or apply themselves inconsistently. They seem uncertain about their level of ambition, although they may dream of great success. When they do achieve success, they may wonder how they got there. They may be drawn by careers that they think will be glamorous or prestigious only to devalue their success once they achieve it. Reveries about the ideal job or career may be consuming and take on a decidedly grandiose coloring. Yet, to the therapist these ideals often do not seem consistent with either skills, talents, or the constraints of everyday life.

Persons with the syndrome of work diffusion have difficulty making distinctions between reality and fantasy or between the work principle and the pleasure principle (see chapter 1). They tend to be dreamers who have difficulty applying themselves to the task at hand. They may dream of a kind of work that bears a strong resemblance to play, but their real work feels boring and tedious.

More careful assessment of these cases in the treatment setting reveals compromised ego functioning. In a general sense, there has been some interference with the "instinct to master." More specifically, there is difficulty sustaining focal attention and in initiating and following through, step-by-step, to reach a goal. Transient enthusiasm gives way to periods of apathy or indecision. The acquisition of skills and the exercise of common sense are either neglected or explicitly devalued. When obstacles are encountered, the tendency is to withdraw and give up.

In many cases of work diffusion, workplace relationships become a primary concern, often at the expense of attention to the tasks themselves. There are strong needs for approval and recognition that are typically not met and lead to feelings of disappointment, disillusionment, and anger. Relationships with coworkers and supervisors can heat up quickly, leading to serious conflicts. As the initial enthusiasm for a particular job gives way to bitterness and cynicism, enemies are made and battles are fought, often destroying the morale of entire departments.

Work diffusion is most common in patients with borderline, narcissistic, and perverse characters. Fast (1975) describes a "borderline work style" with characteristics similar to the ego deficits described above. She hypothesizes developmental difficulties in the transition from early narcissism to objective reality in these cases. These patients have problems modulating omnipotence into a generally accurate appreciation of causal relationships; they cannot modify wishes into realistically achievable goals and make a commitment to the steps leading to objective achievement.

Because doing is identified with the unpleasure world, the sense of identity as a doer is incompletely developed.

Fast suggests two types of family dynamics that can lead to the borderline work style. In some cases the parents, deriving their own sense of aliveness from fantasy and artistic pursuits, support the child's imaginative bent at the expense of her developing skills and an understanding of the parameters of objective reality. At the other end of the spectrum are parents who make demands for realistic behavior that are too extreme and too abrupt, leading the child to retreat from an objective reality that seems to offer little enjoyment.

Stark (1989), taking a self-psychological approach to work disturbance, describes impairments in both intrinsic motivation and the processes of concentrating, focusing, and maintaining a goal orientation that are the hallmarks of work diffusion. He describes patients for whom work is dominated by attempts to repair narcissistic injury. These patients approach a job not for its intrinsic, real attributes, but as a fantasized way of feeling differently about themselves—more alive, admired, and appreciated. Work becomes an idealized selfobject, and the fantasies associated with it confer feelings of completion and perfection that undermine concrete plans and ambitions.

Elsewhere (Axelrod, 1994) I have described a type of work diffusion in male patients that is characterized by intense involvement in work projects that are felt to be unachievable. The content of these "impossible projects" "often involves a grand synthesis or a doing away with ordinary boundaries and categories" (p. 21). They usually entail long-term activity outside the realm of day-to-day work, activity imbued with grandiose fantasies meant to compensate for feelings of incompleteness. I linked this type of work disturbance to developmental failures in the construction of the ego ideal and the achievement of gender identity. These patients, typically having grown up in families with narcissistic mothers and emotionally absent fathers, emerged with a shaky sense of gender identity and an infantile ego ideal. I likened these men's impossible projects to a fetish—an attempt, *based on an illusion*, to achieve a sense of self as an adult man.

Observations made by Fast, Stark, and me suggest some hypotheses about the backgrounds of patients with work diffusion. First, these patients are characterized by problems of vocational identity that are likely to covary with a range of identity problems, including gender identity. Second, as I (Axelrod, 1994) observed in one of my case reports, these patients may well have a higher than average incidence of learning disabilities in childhood. The work life difficulties with step-by-step activity, acquiring skills, and setting realistic goals seem like the adult counterpart of learning problems in childhood. Third, patients with work diffusion were often used as narcissistic objects for one of their parents. Endowed with special needs and expectations by that parent, they were typically protected from the realistic demands and frustrations essential to the acquisition of skills and achievement of mastery.

Patients with work diffusion present formidable challenges in therapy. They typically have severe, long-standing personality disorders that do not yield to short-term intervention. Their grandiosity and sense of entitlement can be off-putting. Their dreamy lack of common sense and avoidance of realistic action can strain the therapist's patience and lead to moralistic attempts to "shape the patient up." Or the therapist, focusing too readily on the patient's changing job or career as a panacea, may miss some of the underlying difficulties. If the therapist sides too readily with the patient's disillusionment and resentment, he will not help build the frustration tolerance that is critical in these cases. Thus, supporting these patients in divisive workplace behavior not only militates against building internal structure, it may exacerbate the work disturbance.

THE PHENOMENOLOGY OF WORK DIFFUSION

Career indecision is commonly encountered in the treatment of patients in their 20s. While Erikson (1950) believed that commitment to a career is fundamental to the achievement of identity in late adolescence and early adulthood, the reality is more complex for many patients with character pathology. Therapists are often faced with patients who have made only a provisional commitment to a line of work and feel undefined and incomplete. These are people who may bounce from one job to the next, unable to find their psychosocial niche and often doing menial work far below their abilities. Typically, in these cases, the lack of self-cohesion becomes painfully apparent after they graduate from college. The structure and protection of the college environment serve a self-enhancing function for these people, and the complexity and openness of the early adult work world can be overwhelming, leading to severe depression, even suicide attempts, that first bring these patients to the attention of a therapist.

Case Example: Jesse M

Jesse started individual treatment in his mid-20s for symptoms of depression and dissatisfaction with his work life. Jesse was unhappy in his job at a publishing company. He found the president of the company overbearing and egotistical, the workplace itself chaotic, and his colleagues workaholics. The entire venture lacked the kind of integrity and authenticity that Jesse had always associated with books and publishing. He knew he didn't belong at the company and felt little commitment to the field at large. He entertained a number of alternate possibilities, none of which seemed very realistic.

Jesse had loved the combination of structure and opportunity for intellectual exploration in college. He found the opportunities to bridge disciplines and synthesize knowledge from different fields to be particularly exciting. He was, however, unsure of his direction after leaving the confines of his small, elite school; the need to commit himself to a specific program of graduate study made him most uncomfortable. Jesse was already depressed about leaving college and the impending breakup of his parents' marriage, when he enrolled in a graduate program in the fine arts. He remembers feeling out of place in the program, unable to connect to his ambitious and unavailable instructors or his competitive peers. When his work was negatively reviewed and he was asked to leave the program, Jesse was devastated. He did not know what to do next and spent the next few years working in menial jobs. Almost five years later, he still felt the rejection and its unfairness acutely.

The roots of Jesse's career indecision in feelings of passivity, helplessness, and an inability to separate from his family of origin soon emerged in treatment. Jesse's mother was phobic and depressed, and he had become strongly identified with her. He felt intimidated by his very successful grandfather, the patriarch of the family, and not adequately supported by his father. His father had built a successful small business that was of considerable interest to his son, but went into early retirement before Jesse could join the enterprise. Jesse was frustrated by his grandfather's overbearing suggestions about what career path to follow and his father's lack of guidance on these matters. He felt excluded from the circle of men in his family and believed that only by starting his own business, as they had, would he gain their acceptance. He found himself waiting for an inspirational idea to come to him.

Jesse used his twice-weekly psychotherapy to focus on work and career issues that were vitally important to him. Early in the treatment, he quit his job in anger and frustration, unsure of what he would do next. He hoped to combine his interests in art and publishing, but his interviews did not lead to a job offer. He became depressed and thought of giving up. He fantasized working as an artisan in a simplified, idyllic setting akin to the protected environment of college. However, with his therapist's support, Jesse persisted in his job search and eventually gained an entry level job in a highly regarded publishing house. It may be that the therapist's growing appreciation of Jesse's deep love of books and its importance as a core element of identification with a depressed mother played a part in the support that Jesse felt during this period.

Now more secure in a job that was a better fit with his interests and values, Jesse's characteristic passivity, frustration, and disillusionment in work life could be addressed in treatment. Jesse's feelings of disappointment with his older male bosses became a major focus of the treatment. He came to see how much he longed for acknowledgment and direction from these men and how quickly he lost the strands of his own activity and direction. These longings were very much what he had felt for a father who had never really understood or fully accepted him. Consequently, he had never fully been able to use his father as a bridge away from his phobic mother to the outside world.

As these issues were worked through in treatment, Jesse felt more independent of his boss's moods and more accepting of the organization's imperfections. He came to see how his own initiatives could add value to the organization and could enable him at the same time to get the training and experience necessary to attain a more desirable position. As he became less invested in vague, grandiose notions of career success, he found that he had more energy to invest in his day-to-day work. Jesse began to grasp the incremental nature of career development and advancement, and it was a revelation for him. He took advantage of opportunities to acquire new skills within the organization and for the first time was able to articulate a realistic, long-term vision for his career. Jesse developed a career path based on a synthesis of his skills and interests and that bore the stamp of authenticity and self-expression. He earned several promotions and began to supplement his salary with freelance work—he had started his own business in his own way.

Case Example: Paul C.

Paul was 27 years old, referred for psychotherapy by his internist because of somatic preoccupations, tension at work, and doubts about his career choice. Since graduating from college Paul had worked in different capacities at a rather large business owned by his family. His commitment to the business fluctuated. At times, he was enthusiastic about bringing technical innovations and enlightened management to the business. Often, though, he felt frustrated and ashamed at not having struck out on his own. He felt that a career in the business had been preordained by his family and was not consistent with his love of children, sports, and the outdoors. He had loved being a camp counselor and wondered if he should have become a teacher, like his brother.

Paul's ruminations about alternative careers most often centered on military service. He had come close to enlisting in the Marines when he was in college and berated himself for not having followed through. He wondered if it was too late and seriously considered enlisting in the Army Reserves. Joining the military was fantasized as a way of Paul's overcoming his feelings of inferiority, vulnerability, and morbid self-doubt. He saw a military career as an unassailable credential, a way of gaining strength in the eyes of others. Paul fantasized that coworkers would take him more seriously if he showed that he was not "just a spoiled kid" but had stood up for what he believed and had served his country. Furthermore, he imagined he would be less vulnerable to ethnic slurs if he demonstrated his patriotism in this way.

Paul's day-to-day work functioning was erratic, and he suffered high levels of stress and tension. Failures in self-regulation were evident in his having trouble getting to work on time, procrastination, and difficulty prioritizing tasks. His reluctance to take breaks frequently led to states of hunger, fatigue, and urinary urgency. Time management was a major problem for him, and he eagerly sought out books, tapes, and workshops that would help him. Paul found it difficult to concentrate, to leave tasks temporarily and then come back to them, and to gauge whether he was putting in enough work.

Paul described a similar pattern of stop-and-start activity dating from childhood. In sports, he failed to perform at points of difficulty and never reached his potential on a number of teams. Although he had been a good student, as an adolescent he became distracted by his social anxiety and compensatory grandiose fantasies. In college, he procrastinated when faced with major deadlines and often completed papers in a panic by working day and night.

At work, Paul wanted people to think there was something special about him, but he dreaded being seen as a member of the owner's family who did not deserve his position and pay. Initially, he felt that he could not possibly live up to his grandfather's and father's reputations but soon became disillusioned with his father's performance. Paul was preoccupied with slights, real or imagined, and was highly vigilant to note the ways that the employees and customers did not take him seriously and were not respectful toward him. He oscillated between permissive and authoritarian approaches to his subordinates but was consistently submissive toward his supervisors.

Paul did not know what kind of role he wanted to play in the business. His need for approval made it difficult to develop and stick with a career path in the business. On several occasions, he would reverse direction to go to another area of the business where there was an immediate need. Consistently, though, he seemed to avoid positions of authority. Even though he had been in the business for more than five years, he saw himself as an apprentice.

The treatment process with Paul was long and arduous. He was caught in a push–pull between his strong dependency needs and his feelings of shame about needing help. Paul experienced being in therapy as a sign of inferiority, and the treatment was punctuated by complaints about the lack of structure in the sessions and his insistence on the therapist's advice and approval.

Paul's anxiety and anger in the face of the special relationship his seductive mother had tried to form with him became a prominent theme of the treatment. He also described a profound sense of having been neglected by his father and of envy of and rage toward his younger brother. Paul struggled with homosexual anxieties and with a constant worry that he was not the strong and manly man that he appeared to others to be.

As in any case of work diffusion, conflicts about choice of career played a prominent role in Paul's treatment. Although he never fully reconciled himself to being in the family business, he did begin to advance and to assume more authority. Accomplishments and promotions tended, however, to be accompanied by an outbreak of psychosomatic symptoms or by a resurgence of interest in joining the Army Reserves. And, although Paul showed an increased ability to sustain focal attention and to work with less stress and tension, he still could not quite figure out where he wanted to go in the business and how best to express his talents, interests, and abilities.

Case Example: Alan B

Patients with "impossible projects" show, most clearly of all the cases of work diffusion, how work can be infiltrated by dream life. The impossible project may be little more than a fantasy, but it dominates the patient's relationship to his work so that day-to-day work is engaged in only provisionally, if at all. When the impossible project is an actual enterprise, it is usually a solitary activity, compulsively engaged in with a kind of timeless absorption. These projects "are imbued with grandiose fantasies. The men dream of being recognized or discovered by a wider audience. The content of their projects often involves a grand synthesis or a doing away with ordinary boundaries and categories. . . . The projects are fantasized to provide an experience of wholeness that has been missing" (Axelrod, 1994, p. 21).

A defining element of this form of work disturbance is that the work project is *felt* to be impossible, whatever its actual status in the external world. These men[2] typically describe a sense of bewilderment about the world of adulthood; they feel fraudulent and subject to crises of self-esteem. Thus, the impossibility of the work project refers to both its tenuous connection to the outside world and to the inherent impossibility of *any* work project's resolving these deficits in the self.

Alan B started treatment in his mid-20s because he was lonely and confused about major life goals. He had been fired from a succession of sales jobs because of carelessness, rule breaking, and conflicts with superiors. Alan felt these jobs were beneath him, and he described himself as unusually intelligent and talented though unappreciated and misunderstood.

Beneath the manifest level of these day-to-day jobs, Alan's work life was organized around a core fantasy of being a performer. He had a dream of becoming a performance artist, which for him consisted of an improvisational, stream of consciousness blending of song, dance, satire, and media with himself as the main character. By the time he started treatment, though, any concrete steps toward reaching this goal had come to a halt. It had already been a few years since he had even ventured out to an audition. Now he only occasionally wrote sketches, improvised "schtick" for his answering machine, and sometimes belted out a song for his friends. He seemed to hope for a kind of dramatic arrival of his one-man show without any plans for how to bring this about.

As a child, Alan had sung and danced in the starring role in his elementary school play. This experience took on the character of a lost dream that he was never able to recapture. Alan felt that when he got older he

---

2. For reasons outlined elsewhere (Axelrod, 1994), "impossible projects" are usually a distinctively male form of work disturbance. In my experience, this continues to be the case, although perhaps not inevitably so.

lost his special relationship to his drama teacher, and without his teacher's encouragement he did not even audition for school plays in junior high and high school. As an adolescent, Alan began to show the same pattern in other areas of his life—early enthusiasm and promise followed by a loss of interest.

Alan had difficulty deciding where to apply to college and remained confused about his academic and career goals. Toward the end of college, he went through an emotional crisis that led him to take a leave of absence and enroll in an acting school. This act of courage, however, was not followed by significant success. Alan felt envious of the other students and angry that he was not more encouraged by the staff. He returned to college embittered but still clinging to the identity of being a performer.

After college, Alan took some acting classes and went to a few auditions. He found both experiences humiliating. He felt unsupported and unfairly rejected by his teachers, and alienated from peers, whom he saw as cutthroats. He was particularly angry at the beautiful young women who were starting to achieve some fame. This maelstrom of feelings became so overwhelming for Alan that he was unable to take any further action. The dream of becoming a performer persisted, but it had become an impossible project.

While Alan went through the motions of earning a living, his sense of self was invested in his impossible project. On the job, Alan was distracted and preoccupied. His arrogance and problems with authority got him in trouble with coworkers and bosses alike. Yet it was very difficult to discuss these problems meaningfully with him in his therapy sessions. It was as if the impossible project were the only thing that mattered to him, that it encapsulated his deepest feelings about work life. Support for occasional concrete efforts to become a performer also had little effect.

Alan's work functioning did not change appreciably until the underlying dynamics of his impossible project were analyzed (Axelrod, 1994). His impossible project served the function of a fetish; it provided him with an illusory sense of his own effectiveness and masculinity. Thus, it could not be given up until the developmental factors contributing to his shaky gender identity were explored in treatment. He had hungered for a closeness to his father that would simultaneously give him a solid sense of his masculinity and help him extricate himself from the world of an unstable and engulfing mother. This longing for a father whom he felt to be unavailable resulted in a combination of compensatory grandiosity, dependency, and anger. These traits were repeatedly played out in his work life.

Only when the early traumatic identification with his mother and long-ing to identify with and be loved by his father were worked through in the transference, in homosexual activity, and in the workplace was Alan able to restart his vocational development. His impossible project eventually became less salient, and he entered a period of true vocational indecision. Soon after entering into his first sustained heterosexual love relationship, Alan made a real commitment to a new field of endeavor. In his new career, Alan was able to synthesize his technical abilities with his needs to charm people and win their approval. While his dependency and egocen-tricity continued to affect his work functioning, these traits were more accessible to analysis as Alan's impossible project gave way to a more realistic commitment to work.

6

Disillusionment and Disability

A s I have noted, normal work life serves a reparative function. Overcoming obstacles identified with "bad objects, bad impulses, and bad parts of the self," enables a person to restore a personal sense of wholeness. In many cases, however, the reparative function of work either is not established or breaks down. When obstacles loom large in a person's work life and failure becomes identified with bad aspects of the self, a debilitating work disturbance can occur. These are cases in which depression is strongly linked to work functioning. Failures in work life can trigger depressive episodes, and depressive thoughts and feelings may center on the person's work life.

The distinguishing feature of this form of work disturbance is an inability to mobilize inner resources to engage work life. Unlike those with a work inhibition who are industrious and committed though relatively unproductive, these patients typically feel apathetic and lacking in energy, unable to recover from setbacks and failures, and ready to give up. Withdrawal, feelings of victimization, phobic avoidance, and, in extreme cases, a demand for restitution are characteristic of these depressive conditions.

The link between depression and work functioning is a costly one not only for the individual but for society as a whole. Depression may result in a person's functioning far below his capacity or even in an inability to work altogether. It may explain a failure to enter the workforce in the first place or may be responsible for later unemployment or disability. Depression in work life is manifested in crippling dependency.

An inability to work that has its onset in early adulthood is associated with emotional and skill deficits that can be intractable. This condition constitutes a profound challenge to anyone trying to ameliorate it, from policy makers to counselors. It requires intensive efforts beyond individual therapy (e.g., specialized training programs; see chapter 9).

The focus here is on those cases characterized by a deterioration in work functioning. This deterioration may result in either episodic and remediable unemployment or underemployment or in a more permanent inability to work. In either case, the dynamics are similar. Rejection, failure, or injury in work life activates primordial malignant self- and object representations that constitute the original depressive core of the personality. The resulting impoverishment of the self and regression to dependency lead to a collapse of initiative, ambition, and goal-directed activity.

Although disillusionment and disability in work life can occur at any point in the life cycle, they are typically functions of workplace experience, unfolding over time and clustering in middle age. For this group of patients, the sheer energy and normative grandiosity of young adulthood begin to erode in the face of obstacles and failures. Without good introjects to draw on, the frustrations of work life lead to depleted energy, withdrawal, and, most important, anger and bitterness. Feeling helpless and unable to meet goals and formulate new objectives, these patients feel that work life is dominated by "bad objects"—personal vendettas, illegal schemes, malingering. Disillusionment with work and career leads not to a recasting of ideals and goals but to traumatized withdrawal and giving up.

DISILLUSIONMENT

Kets de Vries (1978) described a type of work disturbance characterized by apathy, difficulty taking initiative, helplessness, and excessive demands on others in the workplace. He hypothesized that these patients had suffered a disproportionate degree of loss and severe disappointment early in life. He believed that, for these people, the autonomy and independence associated with work trigger a fear of being victimized and lead to withdrawal into helplessness, ignorance, and idleness.

I would add to Kets de Vries's description the central role of rejection sensitivity in these cases. Corresponding to early experiences of loss and disappointment are childhood feelings of being rejected, shunned, different, and inferior. Consciously, a person may hope for a kind of salvation through work; he may imagine that success in work life will alleviate these feelings. Unconsciously, though, efforts are undertaken with the expectation of failure. When hopes for success are not fulfilled, the person finds confirmation that the world is barren and depriving, and he withdraws further.

In these cases, disappointment and disillusionment in work life drive a depressive decline that can be difficult to reverse. The initial hopes and dreams attached to working appear in retrospect as desperate maneuvers to keep a depression at bay. As the person fails to keep successful ventures alive and to get some emotional sustenance from work life, this brittle façade begins to crack. Work life becomes dominated by an unconscious sense of destructiveness and becomes severely compromised. Underemployment and periods of unemployment may result.

Case Example: John R

John, a 55-year-old man, had been depressed for most of his adult life in spite of many years of psychiatric treatment. His work life, once a source of pride and hope, had become suffused with disappointment and bitterness. These feelings about his work both reflected and aggravated his depression. He desperately wanted to make changes in his work life and periodically made efforts to do so, but he had begun to feel that everything he attempted led to failure. He had become deeply identified with the failure of his work-related ventures.

The child of a depressed mother and alcoholic father, John had shown promise in school but had been considered an underachiever. However, he did attend college and in his 20s worked in a Great Society program. This was during the late 60s and early 70s, an exciting time for young people like John who were committed to social justice. He became knowledgeable about his field and took on some supervisory responsibilities. He formed close relationships with colleagues who had similar values.

In his 30s John left the familiar and structured world of his agency and enrolled in a Ph.D. program. He was trying to move from the front lines of organizing to study the theoretical underpinnings of his work. John had difficulty, however, making the transition to the academic world. He was unprepared for the level of competition in his program and felt alienated from his fellow students. He began to resent the lack of support from his professors, and, after encountering some obstacles to carrying out his dissertation project, John became depressed and dropped out of the program. His marriage failed soon thereafter.

Now 40 years old, John moved to another city to make a new start. He planned to put his antipoverty experience to work, this time as an independent consultant on personnel issues. John went through a period of unemployment that further eroded his confidence. He developed some friendships, had a relationship that did not work out, and got enough work as a consultant to scrape by. When a recession hit the area, however, and work became harder to get, John accepted a full-time job and returned to his home town.

John was 50-years-old, alone, and demoralized when he restarted individual therapy. As a line worker in a government agency, John felt that he was no better off than he had been 20 years earlier. Although his boss seemed to respect him and gave him leeway to start new projects, John minimized the opportunities. He envied his boss and was extremely frustrated by bureaucratic obstacles. He tended to be mistrustful of his peers and had difficulty establishing strong working relationships. His irritability and propensity to anger seriously damaged his reputation in the workplace.

John tried to restart his consulting work, but invested each contact with desperate hope and subsequent disappointment. He became enraged when potential clients passed him by and hired others who he felt were no more qualified. Over time, he became more bitter and resentful, and his efforts became more half-hearted.

Thus, by middle age John had moved quite far from the work role and environment that had been a source of pride and strength for him in his 20s. This very dependent man had tried to shift into new work roles that put a premium on independent functioning, a willingness to compete, and a tolerance for rejection. John continued to invest his work life with powerful rescue fantasies; he looked to success as a consultant to validate and vindicate him, to deliver him from the ranks of ordinary workers. Unconsciously, John had endowed his work life with a search for the nurturance he had never gotten. Invariably, though, he ended up reexperiencing the traumatizing, depriving world he had grown up in. John was forever being disappointed.

Antidepressant medication and supportive psychotherapy were ineffective in countering the depletion of inner resources that John experienced. Much as he compared the dead end of his current work life with better times in the past, he compared his therapy unfavorably with previous treatments. He viewed his therapist as not warm and giving enough and held out his lack of career success as proof of the ineffectiveness of the treatment. Sessions became dominated by feelings of hurt and resentment about ill treatment in his family of origin as well as in subsequent relationships, including the one with his therapist. By this time John could see little that was positive in his life or in his therapy, and the therapist had the impression that the treatment, like John's work life, had fallen under the sway of powerful destructive urges. Efforts to resolve the negative therapeutic reaction were unsuccessful, and John eventually decided to look for another therapist.

THE INABILITY TO WORK

The inability to work is the final common pathway for some depressed and severely character disordered patients. For them, stress, whether endogenous or exogenous, can precipitate a shift from a relatively stable, albeit impaired adaptation, to an inability to work. Among the most common endogenous stressors are illness and injury, the process of aging itself, and the failure to achieve career milestones. Exogenous stressors include being fired or the elimination or downgrading of jobs due to workplace restructuring.

There is, then, a psychologically fragile segment of the population for which stress leads to either a temporary or a long-term inability to work. These typically are persons who begin their work lives sensitized to failure and rejection. They react to the inevitable setbacks of work life with some combination of confusion, frustration, anger, and demoralization. The cumulative experience of the world as rejecting and confusing leads to an intensification of passive wishes to be taken care of. Major stressors shift the balance to a refusal or inability to work. These are the people who seem to confirm Freud's (1930) belief that there is a "natural human aversion to work" (p. 80).

The inability to work denotes a person's *experience* of being unable to work. These patients feel that they lack the energy to engage in work life, and they expect failure and disappointment if they do. Over time, they may come to feel that work itself is useless and show an indifference to future consequences. In nonpsychotic cases it may be difficult to untangle the effects of characterological depression, poor motivation, personality conflicts, the secondary gain of unemployment, and a lack of opportunity. The clinician may find it difficult to evaluate the patient's capacity to work.[1] He often does best to assume that the patient's experienced

---

1. These cases typically challenge the therapist to clarify his values with regard to work and to think through when and to what extent to convey to the patient that work itself is beneficial.

inability to work conveys something valid and important, if not literally true, about the patient's current mental state. The meaning of the patient's experienced inability to work then becomes the focus of therapeutic exploration. It can take time in therapy to help the patient understand his reactions to the major stressors of work life, including feelings of anger and entitlement, a profound sense of failure, feelings of worthlessness and helplessness, and phobic avoidance of work itself. The therapist's patience, along with a careful titrating of support and confrontation may help the patient overcome an inability to work.

Case example: Gail M

Gail's work history was already markedly uneven by the time she started therapy in her late 20s. After college, she had had some initial success in an entertainment field, but boredom and dissatisfaction led her to change jobs several times. Then, for several years, Gail tried to work as a freelancer but had difficulty finding work. At the time she started therapy, Gail had taken a low-level staff position doing work she didn't like with people she didn't respect.

Gail's fears of being fired turned out to be well founded. Although she had emphasized her boss's unfairness, the therapist surmised over time that Gail was terminated in part because she did not work hard enough and because her dislike of the job was evident to all. She was quite devastated and was not sure of what to do. She thought of going to graduate school and considered several alternative careers. She even went to a career assessment institute but could not integrate the results of the testing. One thing seemed certain: she would not work again in the same field.

Gail was unemployed for six months before she could even consider looking for work. Her therapist came to appreciate that this "moratorium" gave them the opportunity to understand her anger at being fired and the hurt that made it so difficult to even look for work. Eventually, Gail was able to acknowledge her contribution to the problems on the last job and to face some of the past mistakes that had led her career off-track.

Gail eventually got a part-time, semiskilled job. She liked this job because it was so undemanding and her coworkers were supportive. She built the confidence to work again full time, and, although the job was unchallenging, she was proud that she did it competently and could start to pay her own bills again. Interpersonal difficulties on the job, especially problems with authority, were addressed in therapy and gave Gail the confidence that future difficulties didn't have to lead to termination. She started to look at some of her old work and "remembered" that she had been good at what she did. She began to send out job inquiries and risked going on interviews. After turning down some possible job offers and further refining what she wanted to do, Gail got a job in her original field. It was almost a year since she had been fired, but she had landed the best position she had ever had.

With patients who experience the inability to work, therapists often confront antisocial personality trends. These trends may be primary, leading to the deterioration of work functioning and the eventual inability to work. Such cases were described by Kets de Vries (1978) under the rubric of the "rebellious position," in which the patient has marked difficulty controlling aggression and develops antagonistic relationships with authority. Kets de Vries postulated that the family backgrounds of these people are characterized by excessive parental rejection and frustration combined with an absence of parental control. This family constellation leads to anger toward authority, decreased motivation for compliance, and impairments in the development of internal constraints, frustration tolerance, and foresight. Thus, work is experienced primarily as a demand imposed by authority, and obstacles in reaching goals are attributed resentfully to those in authority.

In the "rebellious position," work life is experienced in terms of coercion and victimization. Paranoid and explosive trends are not uncommon in these cases. Over time, the rage toward authority can have a disorganizing effect that leads to withdrawal from work. In some cases, litigiousness and a series of attempts to "beat the system" may be brought into play to slow the decline into abject helplessness.

These cases are very difficult to treat and challenge the therapist on a number of levels. The patients typically try to draw the therapist directly into their struggles with work, insisting that she support their disability applications and lawsuits. The therapist, in response, must confront her own assumptions and values about work and often feels in an uncomfortable position—between the scylla of excessive gratification of dependency and the charybdis of harsh moralizing about the need to work. Conflict over fees, missed sessions, and the like are common. These are patients who, broadly speaking, have difficulty with the work of therapy (see chapter 7). They tend to develop anaclitic, even parasitic, transferences but lack the ego strength to work them through. Both therapist and patient may soon find themselves wondering if there are any goals at all to the treatment.

When working with patients in the rebellious position it is important to maintain a longitudinal perspective and carefully reconstruct the onset of the inability to work. Patients with primary sociopathy usually do not engage work life or therapy in any meaningful fashion. Patients with anti-social *trends*, however, may periodically experience an inability to work but may respond well to treatment. In these cases, an effective mix of confrontation and encouragement, of individual and group approaches to work-related problems, may be the fulcrum for personality change. With still other patients the therapist may be faced with antisocial trends that are secondary to (rather than causative of) a long-term inability to work. A borderline or depressive who suffers a breakdown may circumscribe his life so much that he loses the ability to meaningfully engage work life, even with the help of treatment and rehabilitation. Such patients become increasingly marginal over time and take on common characteristics of the marginal role: mistrust of authority, a determination to "get whatever I can get," and so on.

Case Example: Joe T

Joe started psychotherapy at age 35 for symptoms of depression, after several previous unsuccessful attempts at treatment. He had moved to the city six months previously, had few social contacts, had not looked for work, and had become suicidal and practically housebound.

Joe was a bright man with good skills but an uneven work history. He was fluent in several languages, had earned a master's degree, and had worked for 10 years as a teacher. Conflict with the administrations of these schools had cost him several jobs, and he was filled with resentment toward those authorities. Eventually, he stopped working in the field altogether and took a clerk's job for a few years. Conflicts with other employees led to the loss of this job too and precipitated his move to a different city.

Joe's parents had a history of alcohol abuse and severe marital discord. The patient described his mother as intrusive and overstimulating, repeatedly attempting to enlist him in an alliance against his distant father. His father was a "redneck" who berated his quiet, sensitive son. As a child and later as an adolescent, Joe was self-conscious and socially avoidant, retreating into a world of fantasy. Later, as a college student, he began to use drugs and alcohol quite heavily and engaged in perverse and promiscuous homosexual activity.

At the outset of treatment, Joe insisted he was disabled and could not work. He was disgusted with "the system" and with the whole idea of working for a living. He wanted to be certified as disabled so he could devote himself to work at home that had all the characteristics of the impossible projects described in chapter 5.

Thus, after years in the "rebellious position" Joe's work functioning had deteriorated significantly. By the time he began treatment, antisocial trends were much in evidence. He felt unable to work in any traditional sense, and looked to treatment to certify him as psychiatrically disabled. Knowing that the patient could initiate such an application and obtain the required examination on his own, the therapist decided not to take a position for or against the issue of disability. Instead, he emphasized the importance of treatment and the treatability of Joe's condition. The therapist strongly recommended individual psychotherapy and evaluation for adjunctive day-hospital treatment.

Joe accepted the treatment recommendations. He made good use of twice weekly psychotherapy and attended a day-hospital program for a year. During that time, his anger and depression decreased, he became actively involved with other patients, and he assumed a leadership position in the program. Eventually, Joe was ready to look for work and, with some assistance from a public agency, found a job as an instructor.

The final six months of Joe's treatment focused on his work adjustment. He was able to work through some of his rage toward the school administration for their greed and disorganization and began to accept that the school's mission was to teach students *and* to make money. Joe learned to focus more on the teaching, which he found rewarding, than on the interpersonal problems that had always distracted him in the past. Joe felt that treatment had been successful and terminated at the point he would have had to begin paying a fee. Chronic characterological issues, including antisocial trends, while far from resolved, were significantly ameliorated. In all spheres of his life, Joe was functioning better than he had in years, although the prognosis for Joe's long-term work adjustment still seemed guarded.

Case Example: Michael B

Michael had been born out of wedlock and was neglected and abused in a succession of foster homes before he was adopted at age five. He grew up as an only child who felt close to his self-sacrificing and overprotective adoptive mother, but distant from his withdrawn, hard-working father.

Taking a series of temporary assignments and moving from plant to plant, Michael worked for almost 10 years in manufacturing. He preferred this kind of work because it enabled him to avoid the conflicts with authority that invariably arose if he stayed in one place too long. He always worked the "graveyard shift" because he felt the atmosphere was calmer with fewer people (especially plant authorities) there.

With automation and cutbacks in his industry threatening the eventual elimination of Michael's job, he decided to pursue his dream of an acting career. He enrolled in acting school, did temporary clerical work, and eventually moved out West in the hope of getting some work in film. However, this first attempt to separate from his parents and live on his own ended in disaster. Michael moved back home, became depressed, and made a suicide gesture that led to a brief hospitalization.

After this collapse, Michael's world became even more constricted. He was certified as psychiatrically disabled, and his life became characterized by long stretches of idleness. Occasional tentative efforts to use talents and skills were interrupted by episodes of profound withdrawal. While unhappy, Michael felt relieved that he did not have to be around people and did not have to deal with the expectations of employers and bosses. In some respects he felt in control and "above the fray"—contemptuous of the corruption, compromise, and lack of concern for others that he saw in people's efforts to get ahead.

As treatment unfolded, Michael's lethargy and inability to sustain goal-directed activity became understandable as "negative symptoms" of a profound regression to a passive, merged state. The "positive symptoms" of this state consisted of interlocking fantasies of his mother's goodness, his father's ineptitude, his own purity, and his eventual success as an actor. Michael could not take action in a dangerous outer world; he felt safest at home in bed.

As Michael's treatment progressed, his brittle, narcissistic mode of relating to others began to soften. Symptoms of social anxiety began to emerge more clearly, as if he were beginning to reexperience early fears of moving out into the world. Michael's lethargy and isolation began to lessen, and he began to date for the first time in almost 10 years. Still, he remained on disability payments and was far from regular employment after several years of twice weekly psychotherapy. The workplace had become associated with the ruthless environment of Michael's infancy and childhood. The disability check had become a source of protection and thus a central organizing force in his life. Michael was unwilling to jeopardize the safety and security it represented. Although he had worked in the past, he had reached a new equilibrium after his breakdown that did not include sustained and focused work in the foreseeable future.

7

Work and the Treatment Process

When we turn our attention to work and the treatment process we are faced with the quandary that although improvement in work functioning is frequently cited as evidence of a positive therapeutic outcome, we know little about how this actually occurs. Soccarides and Kramer (1997) have suggested that psychoanalysts have historically assumed that work difficulties would resolve themselves when conflicts and defenses were fully and appropriately analyzed. This viewpoint implies that analysis takes place separate from the consideration of the patient's work life. I agree that this attitude begs the question of how changes in work life occur through treatment; it also reflects a mythology about psychoanalysis that has not served us well and has become increasingly outmoded. It underestimates the degree to which clinicians actively wrestle with problems in their patients' work lives and want to deepen their understanding of these problems. By not actively engaging important issues in the treatment of work-related problems, we leave the field open to more behavioral, "cookbook" approaches.

My purpose in writing this book is to help psychoanalytic clinicians think more comprehensively about their patients' work lives. In this chapter I focus on how the clinician can turn this increased familiarity and understanding of work-related issues to advantage in the treatment process. As we experience increased pressure to provide focused, results-oriented treatment, we need to articulate better how we leverage our understanding of core personality dynamics to effect change in specific domains of functioning such as work. I try to show how we do so, using what we know about assessment, supportive and exploratory interventions, and the treatment process itself as a form of work.

77

My goal here is not to provide technical instruction so much as to convey a way of approaching work-related issues that is consistent with and enhances the rest of what we do in psychoanalytically oriented treatment. In chapters 3–6 I noted some of the problems that arise in treating specific forms of work disturbance. In this chapter, I, for the most part, eschew the idea of discrete treatment approaches for specific types of work difficulties. Rather, I want to convey the range of effective intervention in the rich material our patients present to us about their work lives.

Drawing on my experience with work-related issues, I have come to believe that there is an irreducible capacity for mature pleasure in work life that is a touchstone of adult development. All forms of work disturbance represent some interference in the satisfaction that *can* be achieved from working. The treatment process is based on intervention to identify the sources of this dissatisfaction and to further the patient's mature pleasure in working. Successful intervention requires the clinician to go beyond pat ideas of success and productivity to address the ways in which working is represented in the patient's mental life. Conflicts and deficits that emerge in the patient's work life are seen in relation to core personality dynamics. The clinician uses a flexible, individualized frame of reference; focusing, for example, on problems with aggression, guilt, values, and ideals as the case requires.

The treatment of a patient's work-related problems is most effective when informed by a developmental approach. The clinician not only formulates the major factors interfering with satisfaction in working, she also begins to think about specific changes that will constitute progress along an adult developmental line of working. She develops a model of change in work functioning for each individual patient. At the same time, the clinician relates these core themes of work life to the central developmental problems of the patient's life overall. This process adds specificity to the understanding of central personality dynamics while connecting work functioning to functioning in other areas of life.

Although the developmental model may be different for each patient, some of the common scenarios that emerge in the early stages of therapy and guide the treatment of work-related problems may be illustrative. For example, a work inhibition characterized by anxiety about competition and assertion is identified by patient and therapist as an important manifestation of a core oedipal conflict. Work functioning has constituted a kind of compromise formation, characterized by passive withdrawal, on one hand, and a mixture of grandiosity and entitlement on the other. As these characteristics of work life are identified and the patient begins to understand how infantile fears and fantasies infiltrate his work life, he becomes more capable of the healthy exercise of aggression, which is a sine qua non of mature working. As the patient relinquishes these infantile fixations, the anxiety and frustration that have characterized work life decrease, and he becomes more capable of focal attention and concentration. He becomes better able to engage work life on its own terms, obtaining pleasure from the reality of work life rather than from the neurotic fantasies that were evident in withdrawal and compensatory grandiose fantasies.

Another patient may have a very different problem harnessing aggression in her work life. The clinician may determine that this patient has marked difficulty balancing her ambition and drive toward a goal with an appreciation of the reality of other people's needs. As a result, she alienates people in the workplace and does not advance in a way commensurate with her talents and abilities. In treatment, these work-related problems might be seen in relation to core conflicts over trust, control, and the management of anger in the family of origin. In a case like this, intervention to shift the balance in work life from narcissism to a more thoroughgoing appreciation of the importance of others can play an important role in resolving a major personality disorder.

In yet another case, the therapist may determine that work-related problems revolve around the absence of guiding values and ideals. Throughout his life, the patient may have experienced a lack of self-cohesion, as evidenced by low self-esteem, an excessive need to please others, and an overall indecisiveness. The absence of maternal warmth and empathy, coupled with parental emphasis on achievement at the expense of relatedness, emerge as central problems in this patient's development. The therapist helps facilitate a deepening sense of the connection between work and the self as an important avenue for self-definition and self-expression.

ASSESSMENT

Assessment is a dynamic process that takes place over time with regard to both the patient's current workplace functioning and her history.[1] It is

---

1. In typical psychotherapy cases, the assessment of work-related problems is not carried out through specialized techniques and does not constitute a discrete stage of treatment. When the patient is referred for clinical career counseling, however, the clinician does carry out a focused, explicit assessment.

critically important that the therapist immerse himself in the patient's work life. Doing so often means obtaining information about the tasks, processes, and personnel that characterize the patient's workplace. The therapist should be familiar with what the patient does at work on a day-to-day basis and should develop an internal schema of how the patient's work role might be filled differently by coworkers. The therapist should also have some sense of the culture and values of the patient's workplace and of the level of morale and reasons for it. These are details that are commonly eschewed by clinicians as derailing the treatment from "more important" emotional matters. They are essential, however, to determining how the patient obtains satisfaction from working as well as the constraints she experiences on obtaining such satisfaction.

The assessment process includes an evaluation of the meaning of work in the patient's family of origin. This is a topic that is also frequently neglected in psychotherapy. The therapist constructs a picture of the skills, aptitudes, and kinds of work done by the parents. He pays special attention to periods of advancement and setback in the parents' work lives, keeping in mind that events that transpired during the patient's adolescence are particularly important in shaping the patient's representations of work. The parents' patterns of interaction around work life are important, as is the degree and quality of the patient's participation in her parents' work lives during childhood. By paying attention to these issues, the therapist is able to develop a picture of what work meant to the patient's parents, how it was used in their relationship, and the degree of satisfaction that the parents derived from their work lives (and thus what they conveyed to the patient).

The dynamics of gender and identification are particularly important in assessing how work life came to be represented for the patient. The meaning of work to the patient is embedded in same-sex and opposite-sex identifications, and the mix varies enormously. We typically think of same-sex work-related identifications as central to a person's gender role identity. However, guiding ideals and values may also derive from either encouragement by or identification with the opposite-sex parent. In such cases, work may become a means of sublimating the erotic tie to the opposite-sex parent. This is one example of how the therapist analyzes the meaning of gendered work identifications.

The case of Gary (Axelrod, 1994) dramatically illustrates the importance of the parental work history in how work becomes represented for the patient. Gary's father had been a successful businessman who retired during Gary's early adolescence, with plans to travel and pursue a number of interests. Shortly after retiring, however, the father sank into a deep depression, was hospitalized, and ultimately killed himself. Gary was paralyzed by rage and guilt and was largely unable to work. Beginning in the early stages and continuing throughout Gary's treatment, he and his therapist joined to reconstruct a picture of his father's work life. Gary remembered his father as having been uninterested in his work, the more silent partner in the business venture. He remembered his mother as having shown little interest in and admiration for the father's accomplishments. However, as the treatment progressed, Gary found evidence that his father had been more effective and influential than his later depression and suicide had led Gary to believe. Gary was able to begin to develop an identification with this revised picture of his father.

In treating work-related problems, the therapist reconstructs the patient's protowork experiences. The capacity during childhood for focused attention and goal-directed effort, as well as early experiences of success and failure in school and sports, are important. Of course, the parents' encouragement of these efforts and their responses to success and failure are part of the picture. The therapist elicits the patient's fantasies and interactions that took place with parents concerning the kind of work he would do as an adult. The therapist also pays special attention to the patient's first work experiences. Especially for woman patients, the therapist should be aware of early conflicts in integrating an unfolding sexual identity with academic and vocational strivings.

If the patient attended college, the therapist takes note of how he chose a major and his general pattern of academic performance. The patient's response to the structure of college life and reactions to leaving that structure must be assessed. For many, this is a difficult passage. Strong pulls back to the protected world of college or family can make it difficult for the young person to move out into the wider world of work. The therapist also develops a sense of the processes by which the patient crystalized the choice of a career and the fantasies attached to the initial career choice.

The therapist's efforts to develop with the patient a coherent understanding of her career path over time serve both assessment and ego-supportive functions. Overall, the therapist develops a picture of how the patient defines satisfaction in work life, the degree to which the patient has achieved that satisfaction, and the patient's understanding of what facilitated or prevented the achievement of that satisfaction. During the assessment stage, the therapist elucidates the patterning of the patient's success and failure, the degree to which she makes use of skills and talents, and the extent to which she takes action to reach work related goals. By communicating early in treatment his understanding of the developmental thrust of the patient's work life, the therapist can help remove blocks to further progress. Throughout the treatment, the therapist refines with the patient an understanding of where she is heading in terms of work, steps that have been or could be taken, and how they might express different dimensions of the patient's personality.

For example, Richard, a freelance producer, was unemployed and significantly depressed when he consulted a therapist in his early 30s. His confidence shaken, he seriously considered leaving this field of endeavor, although he was unsure of another direction. During the initial consultations it became clear that long-standing conflicts related to separation and autonomy had interfered with Richard's career path. He had grown up in a family suffused with conflict, had used drugs extensively, and had been an indifferent student. He worked his way up in his industry and had been able to start a freelance career. However, he tied his career to one major client, and, when that client's budget was cut, Richard was left with almost no work. A regression to dependency ensued, and Richard became abjectly dependent on his wife both financially and emotionally. Reviewing with the patient the dynamics of his career development and its relationship to frustrated dependency needs during childhood and adolescence had a beneficial effect. His lethargy and passivity lifted, he was able to make more focused efforts to find work, and he soon resumed work in his field.

EGO-SUPPORTIVE INTERVENTIONS

The successful treatment of work-related problems hinges on the therapist's actively communicating interest in the patient's work life. The patient may be surprised by the therapist's willingness to become familiar with different aspects of his day-to-day work life. His sense of the therapist's responsiveness to work-related issues may itself have a vitalizing effect on the patient's work functioning. This effect can be enhanced by the therapist's ongoing interest in changes in the patient's workplace and his relationship to his work.

Conveying to the patient that satisfaction and pleasure in working are very real possibilities may have a therapeutic effect. Just as work-related problems are often linked to a lack of parental interest from early in the patient's work life, difficulty in working can stem from a general family belief that pleasure in working is not possible. By articulating a different set of possibilities, the therapist serves an important therapeutic function.

In treating work-related problems, the therapist actively supports the patient's efforts to establish a niche in the work world on the basis of an optimal blending of her unique skills, talents, and interests. From the beginning of treatment, the therapist becomes familiar with the roles and tasks that constitute a patient's work life and develops a sense of the patient's strengths and weaknesses in the workplace. Over time, patient and therapist arrive at a shared language of what the patient is good at and what she aspires to in the world of work. In doing so, therapist and patient begin to define the parameters of self-expression in the workplace for that particular patient. In effect, this constitutes an important component of Kohut's (1971, 1977) "nuclear program of the self." While core skills, talents, and interests may not gain expression through any one job, they may guide the progression of jobs in a particular career.

For example, Jesse (chapter 5) had gotten an interest in art and design from his father's side of the family and a love of books and reading from shared activities with his mother. His first job was in a company that was too driven by ego and technology and too removed from the actualities of books to be satisfying to Jesse. He quit, went through a brief but difficult period of unemployment, and eventually got an entry level position at a company with a reputation for integrity and artistic excellence. Jesse was able to establish a niche for himself at the company as a part-time designer and was eventually promoted to head of the design department. The therapist supported these self-directed efforts and shared Jesse's pride in the unique synthesis he brought about of skills, values, and family legacies.

A patient may turn to the therapist to help decide whether to make a change in his career. The therapist may help the patient determine which options are most consistent with his core skills and values and best support his needs for growth and development. For example, William (see chapter 8) was exploring career opportunities with two distinctly different but well-regarded firms. In one, he would join an established, high profile group where both the demands and the possibilities for financial gain would be great. In the other firm, he would be responsible for the startup and growth of the group; the time demands would be more self-defined, and financial rewards would be more tied to his own initiative. Although a well-placed colleague urged him to take the more secure, higher paying position, he looked to his therapist for understanding of the other values that were important to him—the importance of starting and "growing" a venture, the need for autonomy, and even the excitement of taking a risk. The therapist was able to reflect the importance of these values and to support the patient's sense that he had made significant progress, through treatment, on the outreach and marketing skills that would be essential components of the new job.

Interventions that support mastery and learning play a central role in the treatment of work-related problems. The therapist actively encourages the patient's efforts at mastery, identifying situations in which it has occurred, and supporting or modeling experiences of pleasure in mastery. Identifying the anxiety and frustration associated with work-related learning can shed light on earlier learning problems while helping to improve present-day work functioning.

The therapist actively fosters an atmosphere of safety for work-related learning to occur. This ambiance includes support for the process of active exploration that is so central to work life. Patients with work disturbance are often plagued by rigid and perfectionistic expectations of performance that leave little room for learning over time. They tend to see their efforts in stark terms of success, failure, and iron-clad commitment, rather than in terms of exploring options and opportunities. It is often appropriate to make this distinction clear to the patient and to encourage her to make active exploratory efforts in spite of her fear.

Interventions that focus on the learning process can be invaluable in supporting the patient through setbacks at work. Feelings of helplessness, frustration, and anger can be alleviated by emphasizing that performance on any one task or project is best seen as part of a learning *process*. Without denying the very real disappointments involved in failure, the therapist often does best to encourage the patient to make use of opportunities for learning that emerge from the situation.

Optimally, the workplace facilitates the development of skills that run counter to the patient's neurosis. For example, a rather isolated patient with good technical skills may be informed at a performance review that further career success hinges on improved interpersonal skills. He may be told quite specifically what those skills are. By allying with the patient's need to learn these skills and by appreciating the challenges for that particular patient in doing so, the therapist helps the patient achieve important treatment goals. The therapist may support the patient by emphasizing that these interpersonal skills can be learned like any others. He may facilitate learning by encouraging specific workplace interactions.

The therapist directly encourages the value of activity and assertiveness in work life. Doing so may mean supporting the patient's efforts to reach out and develop a network of contacts either inside or outside the workplace. Or it may mean supporting a request for a promotion, or challeng-ing the perceptions of a colleague or a boss. In cases of disability, the ther-apist may encourage the patient to attempt a job rather than remain idle, especially if she feels that not working will gratify the patient's uncon-scious passive and dependent longings.

Finally, the clinician goes beyond support for the patient's learning and assertiveness to emphasize the value of change, risk, and even excite-ment when it comes to working. In doing so, the therapist runs up against the rigidity and needs for control that constitute the patient's personality disorder.

EXPLORATORY INTERVENTIONS

Self-Esteem

Problems with self-esteem are ubiquitous in work disturbance. In dealing with work-related problems, the therapist confronts either low self-esteem or problems with self-esteem regulation. To help patients develop a sense of success, cope with criticism and rejection, and decrease malignant grandiosity, the therapist uses both supportive and exploratory interven-tions to address issues of self-esteem. These interventions play a central role in bringing about change in work functioning.

Problems of self-esteem in work life invariably lead to exploration of the vicissitudes of the development of a cohesive self. The therapist explores with the patient sources of low self-esteem in his family of ori-gin and in early play, school, and work experiences. The parents' lack of support for and encouragement of the patient's early achievements, as well as their unavailability for idealization, are critical in this regard. Problems developing ideals that are realizable in action and that modulate feelings of inferiority and grandiosity are explored in the treatment process. Tracing the developmental line of the patient's ego ideal while helping him develop serviceable ideals vis-à-vis work life can foster the experience of self-cohesiveness.

While she is exploring developmental antecedents, the therapist con-veys realistic confidence in the patient's skills and abilities. She may actively encourage the patient to undertake a task or job that he fears, and she explicitly acknowledges the patient's success. Over time, these inter-ventions can have the effect of helping the patient remodel his self-image.

I want to emphasize that the therapist's confidence in the patient's capacities should be realistic in nature. Although this may seem to be an elusive goal, I believe that either consciously or unconsciously patients convey an accurate sense of their abilities and performance. Where there are striking omissions (e.g., performance reviews are alluded to but never discussed) the therapist might inquire directly. The therapist over time becomes aware of the patient's tendency either to understate or to overstate his level of performance, and conveys this to the patient.[2] As advocates for our patients' well-being, we are inclined to overestimate their performance; we are reluctant to confront patients with limitations in their work performance. This may be sound practice, but it can be carried to extremes. We do our patients no favor if we expect and encourage a level of performance that flies in the face of their experience; experience that they are reporting to us, although perhaps without registering its importance.

One of work life's greatest challenges is responding appropriately to criticism. Doing so is made all the more difficult by the fact that feedback is so often not constructive or is poorly communicated by the patient's superiors. In such a case, the therapist typically acknowledges the destructive nature of what has transpired and helps the patient work through her anger. The substance of the feedback, however, may be obscured and never accessible to therapeutic intervention.

Many patients are shame prone and have great difficulty even with appropriate criticism. Some are sensitive to any signs of disapproval from colleagues or bosses. The therapist may as a matter of course "reality test" these reactions. She may convey to the patient that feedback and criticism are an integral part of work life and are necessary for learning and growth. The therapist helps the patient to not take the criticism too personally, perhaps reminding him that the feedback is about specific task performance at work, not his overall desirability as a person.

Feelings of shame that surface in the work setting often have their origin in early shame-inducing and often traumatic experiences. These might include abandonment, illness, deformity, or some other sequence of events that left the patient as a child feeling vulnerable and exposed.

For example, Peter S, abandoned by his father at age two, was raised by his mother and a succession of alcoholic and abusive stepfathers. As a child, he was overweight, sad, and lonely. He was teased by other children for being fat and of a different ethnic and religious background than most in his community. As an adolescent and young adult, he used drugs and

---

2. I believe that therapists, in contrast to human resource executives and career counselors, do not pay enough attention to some patients' proclivities to *over*estimate their level of performance.

alcohol extensively, felt alienated from his peers, and drifted through a number of different jobs. While in his mid-30s Peter went back to school to get professional training. After completing school, however, he found it unbearable to be told what to do by his bosses and changed firms several times before starting his own practice. Once he was on his own, Peter's self-esteem oscillated dramatically in relation to his interactions with clients. Relatively minor events—a potential client's not returning a phone call or seeming displeased with his answer to a question—disproportionately affected his feelings about himself. These feelings of vulnerability in relation to real or imagined rejections by clients became a focus of intervention. Their roots in childhood feelings of shame, powerlessness, and humiliation were explored in therapy.

In cases of workaholism work may be a means of *inflating* self-esteem. In these cases, the therapist must always keep in mind the underlying instability of the self and feelings of inferiority and helplessness. Otherwise, she may move too quickly to dismantle the patient's defenses of grandiosity and infallibility, precipitating a breakdown. The therapist should also keep in mind that the pursuit of power and influence in the workplace may be used to shield the patient from feelings of powerlessness and inferiority in intimate relationships. These are cases in which self-esteem can oscillate dramatically, sometimes in conjunction with a mood disorder.

Passivity and Activity, Fantasy and Reality

The treatment of work-related problems often requires the therapist to support steps toward active engagement in work life while analyzing passive personality trends. The therapist typically encourages assertiveness and explores with the patient the sources of shame and guilt that have inhibited such behavior in the past. She does so relative to her understanding of the patient's bedrock level of aggression and ambition. Over the course of treatment, patient and therapist develop a clearer sense of the parameters of the patient's ambition. Encouraging active engagement while analyzing sources of inhibition enables the therapist to help the patient put his ambitions into play while progressively differentiating the patient's from the therapist's level of ambition. (Difficulties in this process constitute a major countertransference issue in the treatment of work problems, discussed later in this chapter.)

A skewing of the personality away from realistic sources of gratification toward wishful fantasy often underlies passive personality trends. From a developmental perspective, this often means that the clinician focuses on preoedipal issues. Merger wishes, early omnipotent fantasies, and the defenses against them are often central to the proclivity toward fantasy in work life. They may be quite ego syntonic, yielding to intervention only slowly and requiring great patience on the part of the therapist.

Thus, passive personality trends are often encapsulated in pervasive and recurrent fantasies with regard to work-related projects or goals. For example, work life may be dominated by unconscious wishes to be discovered by or to merge with the power of a leader, by exhibitionistic or voyeuristic trends vis-à-vis coworkers, by comforting illusions of *eventual* greatness, and by the kind of "impossible projects" described in chapter 5. It may not be possible for the therapist to reduce the impact of these fantasies for some time; identity may be so diffuse and self-esteem so fragile that they are needed to stave off more severe personality deterioration. It may not be possible to challenge these fantasies directly until the patient has acquired more solid skills and a capability for action both within the therapeutic relationship and in the workplace itself.

Bill Y, for example, was a successful junior member of a financial service company. He had earned several promotions and took some pride in his accomplishments but felt uncommitted to his work. For years he had fantasized about starting his own business as the best way of making money to take care of his long-suffering mother. Yet he had little idea of what that business should actually be. Exploration in treatment suggested that these fantasies had roots in early daydreams of being a superhero, daydreams that helped fill the void that had developed in relation to his sickly, depressed, and controlling mother. As these dynamics were interpreted and the patient came to feel less guilty about separating from his mother, he became more engaged in the workplace and its authority and social structure. He decided that the best course of action would be to get an advanced degree and to eventually work as a consultant, drawing on the great value he had always placed on teaching.

A devotion to "higher values" in work life, while sometimes motivating, can also reinforce the patient's passivity. The yearning for "purity" or "creativity" that contrasts to the mundaneness of everyday work may lead to paralysis. Satisfaction in work becomes elusive.

Another patient, Josh A, who worked in an entertainment-related field, depreciated his accomplishments because they were connected to popular taste and commercialism. He aspired to become involved in larger projects that had more artistic integrity and that were not so closely linked with his needs for financial survival. The problem in treatment was not that he had such aspirations but that he was convinced that they were unachievable. The gap for Josh between what he was doing and what he wanted to do did not spur him to action but became a focus for his frustration and feelings of victimization. In treatment, Josh described how he had been invested with many of his immigrant parents' hopes for life in this country. Yet he also felt that he could never accomplish anything that would even come close to his parents' heroic survival of the Holocaust. Alienated from others in their community, the parents struggled to make a living in this country and provided little example of how to make one's way in the world. The patient felt alienated, not privy to how the world really works. He felt entitled to more success, and frustrated that he got so little recognition. As the sources of Josh's grandiose fantasies and strivings for purity were analyzed, he became more adept interpersonally and more capable of the step-by-step action that would enable him to achieve his ideals. He began to feel like less of an outcast, more able to articulate his vision within an organizational structure.

Strivings for purity in work life can lead to an oppositional stance toward pragmatic action itself. Take Bobby P, for instance. After being fired from a job, he was beginning to take some initial steps toward building a private practice in design. However, it soon became clear to his therapist that he was rejecting the advice and assistance of his well-connected friends and was shunning any form of self-promotion. His therapist suggested that Bobby's passivity constituted both defiance toward his successful, older male lover and a way of maintaining an image of himself as innocent, boyish, and needing protection.

Passive patients who define themselves in opposition to the corrupt and impersonal organization they work for often become locked into a kind of power struggle from which they cannot extricate themselves. These conflicts in work life repeat early struggles for autonomy with controlling parents and reflect the patient's lack of confidence that she can stand on her own feet. Although the therapist may grant the validity of the patient's perspective on the workplace, he may focus on the self-defeating nature of the power struggle and the patient's difficulty leaving an obviously bad situation.

Self and Other

As discussed in chapter 1, work life is a critical domain for the ongoing development of self–other differentiation during adulthood. Successful working requires the balancing of narcissistic needs with the reality of others' needs in the workplace. The therapist can be extremely helpful in exploring with the patient the ways in which he has difficulty meshing his needs with the needs of the others with whom he works.

In dealing with work-related problems, the therapist invariably confronts the patient's attitudes toward and styles of responding to interpersonal conflict. The clash of agendas is a given of work life, and it is very important to understand how it is handled by the patient. The therapist pays close attention to whether the patient tends to avoid conflict or to exacerbate it, and with whom and in what kinds of situations. How fearful is the patient of other people and of staking his claim for power, recognition, resources? Interventions may be geared to helping the patient foster an internal model of constructive, resolvable conflict.

Of course, people vary widely in how much they prefer solo versus group work. While temperament, skills, and preferences play a determining role in this regard, the therapist also attends to the ways in which the work activity serves a defensive function. Is the patient who works alone too anxious, suspicious, or angry to work closely with other people? Is the patient who typically works closely with other people anxious about being on his own? For a particular patient, the resolution of work-related problems may hinge on an increased ability to cross over in this regard—from a more individual to a more group approach or vice versa.

Successful working depends on striking a balance between an instrumental view of others and a more personal, empathic understanding of them. We need other people to get the job done, but if we treat them *only* as a means to an end we will foster anger and resentment that interferes with the accomplishment of goals. If we see others primarily as obstacles to our own work, we will not be able to engage their cooperation at critical times. The therapist may intervene to point out such narcissistic dynamics and their negative implications. In doing so, she tries to foster a different sense of how others are "used"—an understanding based on a true appreciation of separateness and a balance between the aggression of instrumentality and the empathy of relatedness.

Trust is a critical issue in work life and becomes a focus of intervention in many cases. Characterological mistrust exacts an enormous toll on workplace productivity, especially as communication and the sharing of information become increasingly fundamental to organizational life (see chapter 9). Maintaining a clear sense of self-interest while establishing collaborative, trusting relationships requires a level of maturity that many patients have difficulty reaching. The therapist explores with the patient the developmental roots of this imbalance and the deeper sources of mistrust. While the therapist does not minimize the patient's need to be alert to threat or danger in the workplace, he also conveys the essential role of trust in getting things done. Helping the patient sort out when to trust and when to hold back in his work life, typically a complex and subjective matter, is a critical means of fostering better object relationships in the patient's life at large.

Issues of Authority

Oedipal-stage issues are prominent in most forms of work difficulty, and interventions focusing on competitiveness and authority are common. Irrational responses to authority in the workplace are the most disruptive influences on the performance of role and task, and exact great costs in productivity and workplace mental health. These transferences reactions readily become a focus of treatment, where they play an important role in the resolution of conflicts related to competition and authority.

Mature working depends on the development of flexible and realistic relationships with figures of authority. The patient must achieve an appropriate degree of separateness from authority figures, as indicated by an understanding of the realities of their power, an appreciation of their real strengths and limitations, and a relative freedom from intense feelings of fear, anger, and love.

For most patients at the beginning of treatment, authority figures in the workplace, like parents, loom large. Fear and awe, wishes for approval, needs to provoke disapproval, shame and guilt regarding competitive urges, and feelings of victimization are common themes in the feelings toward authority. Submissive, avoidant, and combative relationships indicate that the reality of their power is being exaggerated by the reenactment of early parent–child models of relationship.

The therapist encourages the patient's autonomy in work life while analyzing transference reactions to authority figures. The therapist helps the patient keep in mind that while he obviously cannot ignore the reality of authority, he works primarily to insure his own survival and growth not to win the approval of those in authority. The patient is helped to see work life in terms of his *own* developmental imperatives. His relationship to the roles, tasks, and goals of work life is clarified separately from the real or imagined agendas of authority figures.

The therapist helps foster more accurate perceptions of authority figures in the workplace by helping the patient gain a better understanding of what kinds of people his bosses really are—their foibles, strengths, and limitations. It is very helpful, in this regard if the therapist understands the organizational context that affects the boss.

Conflicts with authority are explored by triangulating among relationship patterns in the patient's family of origin, transference paradigms, and current behavior in the workplace. Drawing on an understanding of authority in organizational life, the therapist identifies overvalent relationships with authority figures and elucidates the dominant wishes and feelings that characterize them. The therapist helps the patient make the connection between internalized images of the parents and the operative images of authority figures in work life while helping him develop new scenarios of more flexible involvement with authority. In doing so, the therapist increases the patient's freedom to engage the roles and tasks of work life.

Recall that Anne Z (chapter 4) was driven in her work life to gain the approval of the older male partners and to have evidence that she was special to them. Anne had developed some good mentoring relationships with the senior partners but lived in constant fear that they would find her wanting and favor the other associates over her. The narrowing of emotional focus that occurred as a result of her intense relationship to the current managing partner made it difficult for Anne to evaluate her own performance and decide on her own goals and career path. In treatment, this relationship was explored in terms of the complex longings and fantasies associated with a father who had died when she was six and whom she remembered only vaguely. At the same time, her therapist helped Anne gain a better understanding of the motives and behavior of the managing partner and, after a process of deidealization, to develop a more effective relationship with him.

Alan B (chapter 5) had developed stormy relationships with a succession of bosses that contributed to the loss of more than one job. He wanted to be seen as special by his bosses in ways that far outstripped any realistic expectation. When this attention was not forthcoming, Alan tended to adopt a "bad boy" role that led to reprimands and firings. This pattern of interaction was traced to the patient's relationship with his father, with whom he had used provocative, argumentative behavior to defend against powerful longings for his love and attention. These dynamics were also present in the transference and in transient homosexual activity. Their analysis enabled Alan to divest workplace relationships of these intense needs, to achieve a clearer sense of his own power, and to develop a much more self-directed approach to his work life.

Therapeutic interventions that focus on authority conflicts can help patients resolve inhibitions that prevent them from assuming positions of authority themselves. Conflicts with authority can become a focus for intervention in the absence of an actual work disturbance when the treatment is geared more to career development. Some of the ways in which conflicts with authority can interfere with the full use of potential and the avoidance of a more authoritative position are discussed further in chapter 8.

CASE EXAMPLE

A fuller description of a patient seen in long-term psychotherapy will illustrate how work-related difficulties are treated. In this case, two forms of work disturbance became the focus of psychotherapy and were successfully treated.

Charles G's history and background were described in chapter 4. Family life had been volatile and traumatic. His parents fought often and disciplined the patient and his brother harshly. He experienced his mother as seductive and his father as uninvolved. His brother had had a troubled adolescence, and died of a drug overdose when Charles was in his 20s.

Charles had been an underachiever in school, dropped out of college, and held a series of unskilled jobs before acquiring technical skills and gaining a stable position in his late 20s. Still, when he started treatment at age 35, he felt like a child in the adult world—bewildered and lacking some important knowledge that others seemed to have.

As previously described, Charles initially presented with symptoms of a chronic work inhibition. Although he was responsible and task oriented, his sphere of work activity was quite circumscribed. He was cowed by authority and avoided asking for promotions and assuming authority himself. Typical of the success phobic, any form of self-assertion was unconsciously equated with destructiveness, and he was plagued by guilt. Charles had in many respects, and especially in relation to school and work, gone into hiding.

During the initial phase of treatment, the therapist worked to put a brake on Charles's spiral of depression and self-destructive behavior and addressed profound problems in self-esteem. Exploring the sources of his shame and guilt enabled Charles to take the first steps away from a marginal position in his organization. The therapist was able to help him develop a clearer sense of his very obvious technical and interpersonal skills. Charles came to see that he could take a hand in and enjoy managing people.

The focus of work-related interventions during the middle phase of treatment was to support Charles's ability to learn. He had decided to reenroll in college and initially struggled with old traits of perfectionism and procrastination. Strong transference reactions soon developed toward an older male professor, whom the patient feared, idealized, and wanted desperately to please. Analyzing these reactions to authority enabled Charles to express himself more freely. He completed his course work ahead of schedule and gained confidence in his intellectual abilities and his capacity to turn thought into action. By finally getting a college degree, Charles felt on a much firmer basis as a person. As with many adults who have dropped out of college and are plagued by feelings of being inferior and structurally weak, completing the degree removed a major source of shame for Charles and helped him feel that he was finally being initiated into adulthood.

Soon after finishing his college work but while still basically marking time in his organization, Charles initiated an "impossible project," a book project started during a period in the treatment characterized by regression in the transference, homosexual anxiety, and an upsurge of perverse sexuality. As described in detail elsewhere (Axelrod, 1994), it served the unconscious function of a fetish, patching over ego deficits and providing an illusory sense of masculinity. Narcissistic impairments that became evident in the ideals linked to this project were traced to a traumatic identification with a seductive mother ("the masculine ideal of power") and the devalued image of a passive, though occasionally violent, father. As "wishes to substitute progress on the [project]for the resolution of core conflicts and developmental failures" were analyzed, "[its] aura of impossibility began to diminish" (Axelrod, 1994, p. 27). As the archaic identifications and perverse patterns of relating that attached themselves to the project were worked through, Charles's capacity for goal-directedness and self-expression further increased.

His work on the impossible project had constituted a kind of moratorium or informal sabbatical from his organizational job. With the book completed, he turned his attention back to the job and reevaluated his position in the organization. Although he would sometimes play the role of the director's trusted advisor, Charles came to realize that his responsibility far outstripped his authority. The therapist pointed out that Charles had unconsciously been seeking the director's protection at the expense of a fuller sense of his own authority and leadership. By viewing himself as a "worm" in the organization, Charles was striving for a position of moral superiority by seeming to eschew power and competition.

Charles eventually expressed interest in a new leadership position in his organization. In trying to decide whether to accept this position of increased authority, he had to face the core of his work inhibition as well as a realistic values dilemma. The new position would mean giving up feelings of safety and making more constructive use of his own and others' aggression: it would also mean giving up the freedom to pursue some important cultural interests with his new wife.

After much soul searching and therapeutic exploration, Charles did take the new position. The excitement and pleasure he derived from the job was indicative of a much healthier relationship to work. Charles enjoyed the complexity of the job and the overview of the entire organization that it afforded him. He felt that his work was important to the welfare of the larger organization. He was able to implement his values pertaining to how people should work together and effect change, and he felt that he was quite good at team building and communicating. Charles was surprised at how much time he spent managing others' anger and resentment and how he was able to respond so much more flexibly and less personally to their aggression than he had in the past. He even started to wonder if his mercurial director's occasional put-downs grew out of feeling threatened and if he (Charles) might eventually take over the position of director.

THE WORK OF THERAPY

The therapist's values, experience, and feelings about her own work play a critical role in her efforts to help patients with work related problems. The therapist should understand as much as possible about her own relationship to working. Knowing that this relationship is invariably complex and multi-dimensional, it is optimal for the therapist to view her work with each patient as an opportunity to learn more about her own relationship to work. Each therapeutic dyad constructs over the course of treatment a unique model of what constitutes satisfaction in work life. That model is based on the therapist's own relationship to work, the kind of work done jointly by therapist and patient, and the patient's ambition, skills, conflicts, values, and goals.

Treatment entails an ongoing attempt to understand with the patient his guiding work-related ideals and values without imposing the therapist's own. The nature of therapeutic engagement is such, however, that this is less a starting point than a desired outcome of the process. For it is only by testing out some of his own assumptions about work life that the therapist can help the patient discover what is truly his unique relationship to work.

The value placed by the therapist on ambition and success may conflict with the patient's. With prominent patients, we may get vicarious pleasure from their success but lose sight of the fact that the success may be bought at too high a price. Especially in cases of workaholism, the therapist may be called on to help the patient make work less central in his life, and learn to relax and play more. In general, the therapist should try to get a clear idea of the *patient's* definition of work satisfaction, not assuming that it corresponds to the therapist's. Therapists tend to be high achievers who value success, but our patients may be quite different. We may be more driven than our patients and push them more than they want to be pushed. In these cases, it behooves us to be sensitive to patients' signals that they are not being understood. Thus, we try not to influence our patients toward conventional ideas of prestige and accomplishment if these goals are truly not important to the patients. At the same time, if we feel that a patient is fleeing success, this becomes a focus for intervention.

Differences in values may enter the dialogue between therapist and patient in a myriad of other ways. One person's professionalism can be another's stiffness and formality. One member of the therapeutic dyad may value doing things in teams whereas the other is more comfortable solo. One may emphasize climbing the ladder, the other, "marching to his own drummer." In an analytic treatment, all goals and values, whether the patient's or the therapist's, are subject to scrutiny. As a rule, the therapist should not accept any of the patient's stated work-related goals at face value. The advantage of a depth-psychological approach is the opportunity it affords to explore stated values or goals as a function of early life experience and hence as potentially defensive in nature. The outcome of this kind of exploration can be a sense of satisfaction in working that is based on a deeper understanding of the patient's, not the therapist's, values and ideals.

The therapist's relationship to her own work, both in general and with respect to any one patient, plays a critical role in the treatment of that patient's work-related problems. A therapist's vital connection to her own work provides the basis for an inner model of work life against which the patient's problems can be evaluated and treated. It can serve as a positive example for the patient, although it may also become a focus for the patient's envy and competitiveness.

The therapist's thoughts and feelings about the therapeutic work with a specific patient are also very important. These reactions invariably are conveyed to the patient and help shape his evolving relationship to work life. Does the therapist enjoy his work with a particular patient? What is it that gives the therapist pleasure? When and how does the therapist convey his enjoyment to the patient? Is the therapist's pleasure a pleasure that derives from the work itself or from breaks in the work that may serve a defensive function for both therapist and patient (e.g., the patient's humorous performances for the therapist)? We are accustomed to thinking of the therapist's enjoyment of the work with the patient as an important communication about the self–object dyad. I am suggesting that it is also a powerful communication about the nature of work, and it can have a significant therapeutic impact. This gives the therapist yet another reason to analyze and attempt to remove any obstacles to the enjoyment of his work with a particular patient.

But the practice of psychotherapy is difficult and demanding . Over time, there is great potential for the therapist's neurosis to resurface as cynicism, disillusionment, and the misuse of influence over others. Under such circumstances the therapist may unwittingly communicate to the patient the impossibility of obtaining satisfaction through work life. By colluding with the patient in the belief that work must be drudgery, the therapist may fail to apprehend symptoms of a work disturbance. Alternatively, the therapist's unhappiness in her work life may lead her to overidentify with the patient's successes, thereby failing to analyze a significant work disturbance such as workaholism.

The particularities of the therapist's work life may block an appreciation of the real demands and constraints that affect the patient. A preference common among therapists for security over risk, or for reflection over action, may make it difficult to understand patients who function in more entrepreneurial roles. Similarly, a therapist's emphasis on process over goal may lead to a misalliance with a patient who is accustomed to more results-oriented work.

Therapists commonly choose to work in a private practice because they dislike the constraints of authority, rules, and routine that characterize much of organizational life. But these preferences on the therapist's part do not necessarily correspond to the patient's; certainly they may be in conflict with the realities of the patient's workplace. This disjunction between therapist and patient may enter into the treatment in very concrete terms related to scheduling and payment. Some patients have little say over having to work long hours or travel frequently, both of which will affect the treatment. Such challenges to the treatment frame require flexibility and tact on the therapist's part. The arrangements the therapist makes, for example, in rescheduling appointments, reflect his understanding of the realities of the patient's work life *and* the value he places on therapeutic work. The delicate balance that therapist and patient establish between these two forms of work help the patient better understand the role of work in healthy psychological functioning.

The therapist's responsiveness to patients' work difficulties depends on an appreciation of therapy as both work and play. Following the pathbreaking work of Winnicott, recent trends in psychoanalysis have emphasized a conception of treatment taking place in a "transitional space" or "play space." The free range of imagination in the treatment process and the creative emergence of the self in the treatment dyad do share characteristics with childhood play experience and are important components of treatment. Similarly, as I suggested in chapter 1, there is often (and perhaps increasingly) an element of play in normal working. Therapist and patient may even strive toward a more playful approach to work life as a goal of treatment. The patient may learn to take less seriously the problems and setbacks of the workplace, to rely more on the transformative potential of her imagination to solve problems, to enjoy the absorption in the world of a task or project for its own sake, and to derive pleasure from interactions with coworkers.

But life is both work and play, and psychotherapy is as much workshop as playspace. The therapist communicates to the patient that, while treatment makes use of imagination and creativity, it is also a pragmatic enterprise that leads to real results. With motivation and hard work, intangible and complex psychological problems are ultimately comprehensible and resolvable. That treatment requires hard work helps limit its regressive potential. The therapist who disregards or does not adequately value the fact that treatment is work as well as play may seriously mislead the patient, unwittingly reinforcing passivity and neurotic self-absorption.[3]

Finally, the treatment of work-related difficulties raises the question of the mutative potential of these interventions for the personality as a whole.

---

3. The therapist's keeping clearly in mind the element of work in therapy can be invaluable in uncovering central transference and resistance paradigms. For example, some severely damaged patients who lack an inner sense of viability and agency take a profoundly passive approach to their inner lives. These patients may use therapy primarily as a means of communicating distress. They may come only gradually to appreciate that they can take an active approach to inner experience and thus undertake the *work* of therapy.

While focal intervention in a patient's work life can lead to real improvement in this domain of functioning, the major leverage for structural change in the personality remains the relationship—both real and transferential—between therapist and patient. Work life provides an avenue for addressing the transference in displacement and for revising and consolidating substructures of the personality through content interpretations. Inasmuch as such interventions remain at some remove from the immediacy of body experience and the interactional field of therapist and patient, however, they have a limited relationship to mutative change in the personality. Work life is likely to be most closely linked to personality change through the immediacy of the treatment experience as a workshop, in which a balance is struck between goal and process, work and play, pleasure and effortfulness.

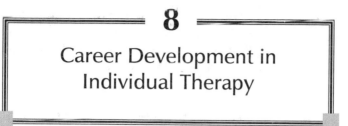

8

Career Development in
Individual Therapy

Therapists are sometimes faced with major concerns about career development on the part of patients whose work functioning seems quite intact. In contrast to patients with a manifest work disturbance, these are patients who for the most part like their work and are not plagued by work-related anxieties and conflicts. They tend to be bright, talented, and accomplished but feel they are not as productive as they would like to be and that certain career goals are either ill defined or elusive.

While the symptoms of a work disturbance may be the precipitant for seeking treatment, career development issues seldom carry with them the same kind of urgency. Rather, as treatment progresses in these cases and the patient comes to expect more growth and satisfaction from life, career functioning comes under closer scrutiny and career development issues can become a more important part of the treatment. These are people who might otherwise receive workplace coaching or seek out vocational counseling, but because they are already in psychotherapy for other reasons, the interested therapist has an opportunity to affect the patient's career development significantly.

In this chapter I use several case examples to outline a psychotherapeutic approach to career development. This approach is a hybrid of psychotherapy, on one hand, and vocational counseling and coaching, on the other. It is based on a psychodynamic understanding of the relationship between a person's personality and the characteristics of the work role he occupies. Treatment proceeds in typical psychotherapeutic fashion by analyzing the conflicts and defenses that have an inhibitory effect on the personality. At the same time, the coaching aspect proceeds with more directive, behaviorally oriented interventions addressing the patient's work life, especially those geared to assertiveness, communication skills, and conflict management. Counseling interventions may include clarification of career goals, and strategizing about how to achieve them. The psychotherapeutic dimension of this approach, along with the coaching and counseling dimension, has a synergistic effect. As personality growth occurs, the patient can risk different behaviors in the workplace, including role redefinition and change. At the same time, coaching interventions, if properly based on a psychodynamic understanding of the personality, bring to the fore central treatment issues and are instrumental in working them through.

This approach to career development has important advantages over traditional counseling and coaching approaches. The therapist does not labor under the same constraints as the coach or counselor in terms of topics she can broach. She can use genetic/developmental material, transference and countertransference data, and information about the patient's intimate relationships to gain a more potent understanding of the patient's career-related issues. She can achieve a more thoroughgoing understanding of the fears and inhibitions that prevent vocational progress and can address in vivo the resistances to implementing change as a component of resistance to treatment.[1]

This approach requires a high level of activity and directiveness on the part of the therapist. The therapist typically offers suggestions about how to handle day-to-day work life situations, although, unlike the typical job coach, she does not directly monitor the patient's follow-through on these suggestions. This high level of activity invariably shapes the patient's transference and puts limitations on the analyzability of some of its aspects. Furthermore, both therapist and patient must guard against the collusive use of this vocationally oriented work to avoid dealing with more emotionally valent and more threatening issues of intimacy.

FUNDAMENTALS OF A THERAPEUTIC APPROACH TO CAREER DEVELOPMENT

The treatment approach I describe is based on an assessment of the dynamic interplay between the patient's personality and the work role he has assumed. The therapist uses her background understanding of orga-

---

1. Indeed, the clinician's ability to address resistances effectively lends unique power to her career development interventions.

nizational life as well as direct questioning of the patient to gain as clear a picture as possible of the demands and constraints of the role that the patient is filling. She must consider both the formal and the informal elements of the patient's role—a sense of the culture of the particular workplace is invaluable. While on-site job coaching makes use of directly obtained information about coworkers, the therapist must rely on the patient's reports. Although this approach admittedly has its drawbacks, the well-trained clinician can still obtain a valuable perspective on the motives and behaviors of important people in the patient's work life and how they affect the patient.

As the therapist learns more about the patient's work environment, she tries to develop a picture of how the patient is filling the particular work role. She asks herself how the patient's specific constellation of conflicts and defenses, deficits and talents has shaped the unique ways in which the patient is living out his work role. In so doing, the therapist disembeds the patient's unique construction of the role from what she understands to be the more essential and invariant demands of the role. The therapist may contrast the patient's construction of the role to what she imagines other constructions of the role to be.[2] Thus, therapist and patient develop over time a scenario of how the patient could fill the role if freed of some of the constraints imposed by neurotic inhibitions. This scenario becomes the basis for interventions.

In this approach to treatment, therapist and patient are continually monitoring the dynamic equilibrium between personality and work role. The psychodynamically oriented clinician is particularly adept at understanding the interplay among personality change, alteration of the work role, and creation of a new work role in a new setting. The therapist may at first work with the patient to redefine the work role in a way that is commensurate with the personality growth that is occurring in therapy. Typically, as the patient becomes more sure of his work-related ideals and values, the therapist supports his efforts to redefine his responsibilities, alter his relationships with bosses and coworkers, increase his compensation, and so on. Not infrequently, though, the familiar bonds of dependency, punishment, and reward must be broken for career development to proceed.

---

2. Although the therapist's alternative constructions of the work role may leave the door open for the imposition of her values, they are not qualitatively different from other ways in which the therapist develops alternative images of role functioning that guide intervention. Optimally, the therapist's alternative versions of the work role are based on a growing understanding of the patient's ideals.

In practice, then, personality change, redefinition of work role, and leaving the specific work role often constitute a sequence. In some cases, the patient can grow and change within a redefined work role; in others, she must leave the role altogether. Either way, helping the patient through this process can be an invaluable part of the treatment.

By focusing on the reciprocal influence of role and personality, the therapist is drawn into the world of the organization. Psychotherapeutic engagement in career development requires the therapist to balance the patient's perspective on the organization with what he knows about the dynamics of organizational life. If the therapist does not have prior knowledge of the patient's field of endeavor—the distinguishing features of its roles, tasks, and culture—he should try to glean them from the patient's material or from other sources. Understanding recent developments in the patient's field can help the therapist to grasp the fit between the patient's personality and his work role. Diagnosing the styles of relating and communicating that are characteristic of the patient's organization can be invaluable in understanding how the patient is filling his particular role. A sensitivity to changes in style within the organization can be used by the therapist to help alert the patient to opportunities to expand and redefine his role in conjunction with ongoing personality change made in psychotherapy.

Mindful that it is acquired through the lens of individual treatment, and thus invariably subjective, the therapist strives to develop a detailed picture of how a particular segment of the organization functions. If the patient occupies a leadership position in the organization, linked changes in that patient's personality and role functioning can bring about significant change in the organization. In select cases, then, individual therapy can affect the overall functioning of the organization and even contribute to changes in the organizational culture.

In the following case, personality changes that took place in psychotherapy enabled the patient to keep up with changes in his field, to reevaluate his role in his organization, and, ultimately, to make a major change in his career.

Case Example: William L

William started therapy in his early 40s because of a crisis in his marriage. After making the decision to work on his marriage rather than seek a divorce, William began to redirect some of his energy to his work life. William had become dissatisfied with his position as the managing partner of a small financial services firm. In spite of his efforts over the previous years, he had been unable to improve the firm's fortunes significantly, and his own financial situation was troubled. Chronically frustrated and angry with the other partners in the firm, he questioned his capacity for leadership and his interest in administration. Partially aware that he had not lived up to his potential and the promise he had shown in school, William was uncertain of his goals and direction.

The therapist concluded from an initial assessment of William's family history and vocational development that characterological problems had blocked William's career development. He was sufficiently invested in, yet troubled by, his vocational functioning so that career development became an important focus of the treatment. William used therapy sessions to discuss in detail his role in the firm and the interpersonal and systemic problems in the organization. He welcomed an approach that combined interpretation of characterological problems with suggestions for new ways to manage interpersonal problems. Ultimately, treatment comprised a thrust toward a more differentiated work identity, with a better synthesis of skills, values, and goals.

William had grown up in an upper middle class New England family that emphasized propriety and responsibility. His emotionally distant mother instilled in him the need to be a "good boy" who made few demands and caused little trouble. His father, a successful businessman, held William to high standards and did not hesitate to "lay down the law." The patient had learned to sneak around his father rather than challenge him directly. Even as an adult, the patient feared his father. William's problems in his family of origin had left him longing for unconditional love and acceptance from a woman while feeling unsure of his place in the world of adults.

William had been an outstanding student, who was somewhat less than enthusiastic about going to graduate school. After graduating, he returned to his region of the country and joined a well-regarded firm. Increasingly unhappy in his first marriage, especially with his wife's unrelenting ambition, he moved to New York. At his current firm, William soon became the protégé of the senior partner. When the "old man" suddenly became disabled, William led a bitter fight against the partner who had taken over. The patient's faction eventually won, and he became the managing partner, but with lingering doubts about how he had handled the situation. He alternately reproached himself for having been too Machiavellian and for having been too easy on his rival.

By the time he started therapy, William had grown increasingly uncomfortable in his role. He preferred immersion in arcane technical problems to having to interact with and manage people. His leadership style was dry and distant, and he tended to communicate by memo from behind a closed office door. At the same time, he had difficulty standing up to partners who challenged him or made unreasonable demands.

Had this been a different era, William might have been a respected, moderately successful professional with limited leadership and communication skills. However, his field had become more competitive, and William soon learned that he had to market his practice in order to survive. Successful practice in the 90s required both skills at presentation and sustained outreach to potential clients. Thus, William had to confront aspects of his character related to his aloofness and problems with assertiveness that he might have been more able to overlook in the past.

As the inhibition in William's work functioning and its origins were addressed in therapy, he began to take steps to develop new clients. Specific efforts in this area were directly encouraged in therapy, and, to his surprise, he found that he was quite good at practice development.

William's role within the firm also became a focus of the therapy. Although he had seemingly achieved a good position, in many ways he had been in hiding. He tended to surround himself with women partners in the hope that they would protect him and support him. At the same time, he avoided the male partners and did little to develop a working relationship with them. His attempts to handle conflicts within the firm were erratic, alternating between an off-putting exercise of authority and withdrawal.

William was encouraged to become less dependent on a female partner whose contribution to the firm was very limited and to communicate more effectively with a male partner who shared administrative responsibility with him. In therapy, William worked on communicating the specifics of what he wanted from the other partners and why. He became less conflicted about using his authority appropriately.

An external consultant who had been brought into the firm independently encouraged William to become a more participatory leader who was more actively involved in team-building. Although the interpersonal problems affecting his role as a leader had been a focus in therapy, he was supported in his conviction that the team-building approach was not the right path. It probably could not make up for the fact that William had made very real mistakes in hiring and that the other partners now had very real liabilities. Denying his potential hires' limitations and hoping for the best from people, William had been unable to bring in people who could really strengthen the firm. His characterological avoidance and fears of competition had impaired his ability appropriately to select people for the firm.

In therapy, William grappled with how much he could change his role functioning, how much he could change his firm, and whether he could look for a better position elsewhere. He eventually concluded that, both because of his own managerial limitations and because of the size and composition of the firm, it probably would never be the kind of work environment that he needed for his career to develop. This realization at first filled him with guilt. He worried that the firm would collapse if he left. But he was also afraid that if he were to leave the safety of the firm he would not be able to compete in the "big leagues." Going to a larger firm where he could more fully develop his area of specialization brought with it a fear of higher expectations and of eventual punishment, whether it be for failure or success.

Ultimately William decided to leave. He obtained an excellent position at a larger firm. He saw for the first time the possibility of living up to his potential in work life. The separation process itself became a focus of treatment. Guilty about leaving and afraid of the other partners' anger, William needed encouragement to prepare the partners for his leaving and to influence them to agree to a better severance agreement. He felt entitled to leave and resented the need to explain the reasons for his actions as encroachment on his autonomy; that is, he could not think about what the other parties to the separation might need in order for the process to go smoothly. William continued to need his therapist's support as he dealt with the stress of leaving what had felt like a safe environment.

Case Example: Jerry S

The case of Jerry illustrates the intricate connections between early development and adult work life. In this case, the patient's role in the family made him seem ideally suited to his work role in the organization. As treatment progressed, however, it became apparent that this repetition of role was both perpetuating Jerry's depression and limiting the development of his career.

Jerry was already married and beginning to achieve prominence in his field when he started therapy for symptoms of depression. His depression was linked to feelings of helplessness and anger in a number of enmeshed relationships. These included relationships with his family of origin, his wife, and his coworkers.

Jerry's parents had separated during his preschool years. He remained quite close to his father, whom he described as a brilliant but troubled man—tense, histrionic, and easily hurt. His mother was chronically depressed during much of his childhood. Jerry was the "fair haired boy" of the family, the one whose role was to make each parent feel better. He was highly attuned to the upsets of each and strove mightily either to calm them or to cheer them up by singing and dancing for them. Although he had fantasized as a child that achieving fame would restore some measure of dignity and status to his family, he felt smothered by his parents' investment in his success. He alternately pushed his parents away and then guiltily drew them close, unaware of how truly conflicted he was about being the family's "savior."

Although clearly very bright, Jerry had been an indifferent student. However, in college he found his true calling in the arts. Talent, hard work, and some early recognition catapulted Jerry to success. By the time he started therapy, Jerry had gained real prominence.

Jerry's work role was a complex one. He was an integral member of an organization and exercised major responsibilities in the creative area. He was the number two man in the organization, and his relationship with his boss was critical for the success of the venture. Jerry described how in his field this relationship was defined and constrained by tradition. An important part of his role was to calm and reassure his boss, to enable him to function on a day-to-day basis.

From the beginning of treatment, Jerry complained bitterly about his boss, D, whom he described as anxious, insecure, insensitive, and megalomaniacal. He felt humiliated by some of the assignments D gave him, and complained of how D's self-centeredness destroyed the morale of the organization. In contrast to D, Jerry stood for treating people well and saw himself as a buffer between his boss and the rest of the staff.

The work-focused component of Jerry's treatment hinged on sorting out how much his role functioning was an organizational given and how much was a personal creation that served neurotic ends. In the organization, Jerry was indeed repeating the role of parentified child. He mollified and reassured the temperamental D much as he had his father. He put the needs of other members of the organization ahead of his own, much as he had done with his mother. He saw himself as playing a critical role in holding the organizational "family" together much as he had his own family as a child.

In therapy, Jerry came to realize that his role in the organization both gratified him and made him furious. He felt superior to D but at the same time felt in his thrall. Jerry's role, as he had interpreted it, made him feel valuable and needed by other members of the organization. This became especially clear when Jerry began dropping hints that he might leave the organization and was repeatedly told how invaluable he was and how he was a much better leader than D.

Early in his treatment, Jerry felt straitjacketed by his role in the organization. He felt that there was no choice but to do D's bidding. After all, D was just acting the way heads of such organizations are supposed to act, and, besides, he was "too far gone" to be able to listen to Jerry's complaints. Jerry's resentment toward D was giving him an opportunity to express, in displacement, his long-standing anger toward both parents. But his very constraining interpretation of his role also helped perpetuate his depressive symptoms.

As treatment progressed, Jerry's therapist began to question his assumptions about his role, especially vis-à-vis D. Times had changed, and it seemed to the therapist that someone in Jerry's role no longer had to demonstrate absolute fealty to his boss. Although Jerry was only peripherally aware of it, D had given signs that he *could* respond to Jerry's feedback and did have some capacity for a more collaborative relationship. The therapist began to encourage Jerry to expand and redefine his role in the organization. For example, Jerry had identified his fear of undertaking his own creative projects outside of the organization as a major therapeutic issue. He worried that D demanded absolute devotion to the organization and would not tolerate his strivings toward creative autonomy. With little concrete evidence for this perception and with the understanding that it was at least in part a projection of parental attitudes, Jerry was encouraged to follow through on some of these projects. D's response was quite favorable. Processing this series of events in therapy, Jerry came to understand that in his family true autonomy was construed as abandonment. Self-directedness, as expressed in carrying out his own projects, was unconsciously viewed by Jerry as selfishness, as turning his back on those who needed him.

As the organization became more successful, Jerry fantasized that D would become more mature and generous toward others. Instead, D seemed to become more insecure and megalomaniacal. Over the course of a few months, Jerry worked himself into a frenzy of righteous indignation. D was a lost cause, he would never change, and there was no choice but to leave the organization sooner rather than later. Speaking to D would only lead to an explosion.

By this time, the therapist had reason to believe that Jerry could assume a different role in relation to D. Jerry's needs *not* to communicate with D and to maintain a polarized relationship with him were discussed with him in therapy. He was encouraged to see himself in active partnership with D and to voice his observations and concerns. Jerry had a constructive discussion with D, in which D was able to acknowledge both his anxiety about his new-found success as well as his problematic behavior. Thus, Jerry had begun to redefine his role. He no longer felt so compelled to soothe and placate D in order to hold the organization together. Although his position carried with it special obligations, they did not preclude his asserting his own values and speaking the truth as he saw it. Jerry had become less enmeshed in his role and more able to be himself. This change left him less depressed and freer to pursue his own creative projects.

Case Example: Kate R

The case of Kate differs from the previous two cases in that she experienced more manifest distress about her career, and her career difficulties were more deeply rooted in the neurotic aspects of her personality. Her career indecision bordered on the kind of work diffusion described in chapter 5, although she functioned quite well on the job. Because her case highlights some of the most important issues confronting women with careers, and because the understanding of organizational role and culture played such an important part in her treatment, the case of Kate will be described in some detail.

Kate, a single woman in her mid 30s, was working in a major accounting firm when she started therapy for problems in relationships and unhappiness with her career. Although she had been in accounting for eight years, she felt that she did not fit into the world of finance. She felt different from coworkers in terms of political opinions, cultural interests, and matters of style. Kate fantasized about a career that was somehow more artistic or literary but could not think of anything more specific and did not know what to do.

The elder of two children and her father's favorite, Kate had grown up comfortably middle class. She felt more in common with her extroverted, charming, businessman father than with her more bookish, emotionally cool mother. While her mother had been particularly critical of her and put out by her rebelliousness during adolescence, her father had maintained a warmer, more accepting attitude. Her parents' marriage had at times been strained, and Kate was sympathetic to her father when her mother was critical and scornful toward him. Kate felt closer to a father whom she unconsciously perceived as available; her relationship with her father was mildly sexualized.

Kate remembered being a very good student who excelled in math at her all-girls elementary school. Everything changed, however, when she went to a much larger, coed, public high school. She lost interest in academics and concentrated instead on being popular by using drugs and cultivating a rebellious, disaffected image. Kate lost confidence in her intelligence, and occasionally cheated on high school exams. At the same time, she idealized her boyfriend's intelligence, and turned to him for guidance.

In college, Kate applied herself inconsistently to her work. When she did well, she tended to attribute her success to a male professor's liking her rather than to any particular ability she might have. She felt that she relied on her ability to charm male professors to make up for her inability to get the work done on time. This pattern continued into graduate school. She felt that she could work hard if she liked the professor and would be rewarded with a good grade, at least in part because the professor would respond to her liking him. She felt that she was much better at making an "anti" argument than at really mastering a body of knowledge. She felt intellectually fraudulent.

Kate remembered having fallen into accounting after graduate school because her boyfriend at the time was in the field. After staying with the same large institution for eight years, she eventually moved into one of its most challenging and prestigious departments. She was one of the only women in her section and seemed to thrive on the attention of her male colleagues. Kate presented herself as "spacey," charming, and provocative and described herself as a "thing," a "phenomenon," in the buttoned-down male world of her department. But as much as she struck a pose of studied indifference to accounting, Kate was terrified that the inadequacy she felt in the quantitative/technical aspects of her job would be discovered with disastrous consequences. Her fear of making even a small mistake in the quantitative part of her job led her to turn too quickly to her male bosses for help instead of thinking problems through on her own.

The vocationally oriented component of Kate's psychotherapy focused initially on the highly conflicted work role that she had constructed. Her feeling that at work she was mostly image with little substance correlated with her chronically low self-esteem in intellectual matters. Kate had first been a "thing" to get her charming father's attention and had felt intellectually inferior to men since high school. Her way of not threatening men and insuring their attention had taken on masochistic features in relationships and, to some extent, in work life also. Her block in the quantitative/technical realm of her job grew out of these feelings of inferiority and needs to submit.

Kate was able to become more confident in her work role but was still plagued by doubts about her field of endeavor. She observed that her father was more excited about her prestigious job than she was and began to wonder how much she had become an accountant to please him. She noted that she hated the long hours of her job, whereas the men in her department prided themselves in the heroic efforts they were making. They seemed to love their work and knew that they wanted to be accountants more than anything. She wanted to feel that she was doing something that was meaningful for society and more consistent with her liberal values. Yet she feared leaving such a high-paying job.

The therapy moved slowly with respect to these issues. Kate had found a way of coping in the "macho" world of her department but increasingly wondered if she wanted to. Her male colleagues seemed willing to give up their personal lives for the glory of prestigious jobs, but she increasingly came to feel that she was not willing to do so. The director of her department even tried to recruit her to a task force to determine why the department had so much difficulty attracting and keeping women, but she was not interested. The therapist observed the patient's increasing sense of divergence between her own needs and values and the immutable features of the work role she was filling. Kate was beginning to feel that she could direct her own career and think for herself rather than continuing to take direction from and try to win the attention of her male bosses.

Kate came to feel that the only way she could fundamentally redirect her career was by leaving her department altogether. Her job was so demanding and compelling that she could not explore alternatives while at the job. Her strategy of quitting was clearly risky, and she was warned against it by her parents. But having gained the courage to strike out on her own, Kate announced her resignation.

Psychotherapy can play a critical role in the job-search phase of a patient's career development. During this period, Kate was encouraged to actively explore alternatives and not settle too quickly for a familiar kind of work that would again be in conflict with her values. Treatment included a continuing focus on Kate's differentiating what she wanted to do from what she imagined the men in her life wanted her to do, and on the roots of her feelings of intellectual inferiority.

CONCLUSION

In this chapter I have used three cases to illustrate how vocational development can be facilitated in individual therapy. I have stressed the importance in all cases of the therapist's having an understanding of the demands of the role and the culture of the organization. Further understanding of changes in the patient's field, and their potential interpersonal and intrapsychic effects, can be invaluable in guiding the therapist's interventions.

As noted in the case of Kate, there is some overlap between the treatment of a work disturbance and the approach to vocational development that has been described in this chapter. Vocational development occurs in the course of treating a work disturbance, and there is often at least a mild work inhibition in cases where vocational development becomes a focus. Thus, although I believe that there are valid distinctions to be drawn, I also view them as being a matter of degree.

The emphasis in this chapter has been on how the development of a sense of work identity occurs in individual therapy. Typically, the patient in therapy comes to understand better how he has filled a work role on the basis of the needs, conflicts, and relationship paradigms of childhood. As he develops an expanded view of the self, he can engage in a redefinition of the role more in keeping with his new capabilities. The therapist can play an important, active part in this process as he thinks through with the patient ways of communicating and interacting differently in the workplace. Helping the patient set new goals can be an invaluable aspect of the change process that occurs in therapy. Ultimately, this may mean helping the patient through the process of separating from a role and an organization he has outgrown.

In all this, the patient's increasingly differentiated sense of his own values plays a critical part. It stands to reason that a more penetrating sense of one's own values evolves during a successful psychotherapy. Optimally, this frees the patient to assert what he believes in and where he will take a stand in his work life. This capacity to use aggression in the service of self-definition is a sine qua non of healthy working.

9

The Psychology of a Changing Workplace

The focus of this book has been on the work life and career of the individual as seen through the lens of psychoanalytic psychotherapy. Little attention has heretofor been paid to the many systems that affect the patient's work life—the work group, organizational culture, technical innovations, and the like.[1] In this chapter, I will explore the broader changes in the economy and the workforce that are affecting the work lives of therapists and patients alike. In doing so, I hope to situate our treatment of work-related problems in a larger context that clinicians typically pay scant attention to.

Powerful and tightly linked economic, technological, and cultural forces are altering the very nature of work itself[2] and thus the personality traits and behavior that are viewed as desirable (F. Doolittle, 1996, personal communication). The aggregate effects on the individual are profound. As clinicians, we are often confronted with patients' difficulties adapting to underlying changes in the nature of work. Our patients are subject to

---

1. Understanding and influencing these systems are the objectives of organizational consultants, some of whom combine psychoanalytic and systems approaches (Miller and Rice, 1967; Kets deVries, 1983; Hirschhorn, 1988). The clinician who is interested in work-related problems would do well to familiarize herself with some of this literature.

2. Whether this situation is unique to the current period, as many theorists suggest, or whether work itself is a constantly changing and evolving human experience, is not clear. Whatever the case may be, the goal here is the same—to map the dynamic relationship between the changing workplace and personality functioning.

layoffs, reorganizations, takeovers, and the anxiety that accompany them. But there are more subtle and longer term changes that also affect all of our work lives—shifts in the norms and values of a profession, changes in the employer–employee bonds in organizations, and so forth.

THE CHANGING WORKPLACE

The New Economy

Just as the culture of the late 20th century has been labeled post modern, our economy has been variously described as postcapitalist (Drucker, 1993), postentrepreneurial (Kanter, 1989), or postindustrial (Hirschhorn, 1988). Changes in the economy have been driven by revolutionary developments in production and information technology and by the globalization of enterprise. According to Peter Drucker (1993), although 90% of the American workforce was involved in "making or moving things" in the early part of this century, only about 20% of the workforce was involved in such activities by 1990. That number is expected to decrease to only 10% by the year 2010. Drucker argues that the basic economic resource is no longer either capital or labor but knowledge—value is created by the application of knowledge to work. Fully one-third of the workforce in developed countries are knowledge workers, and their importance will only grow with time.

Rosabeth Moss Kanter (1989) has described the postentrepreneurial economy as characterized by "more opportunities along with more competition, more activities to manage, and more limited resources" (p. 23). She argues that technology has opened new business opportunities and that technological breakthroughs can come from anywhere in the world. There is increased competition for global markets. Kanter emphasizes that "activity proliferation" is an important characteristic of the postentrepreneurial economy. There is an increasing volume and a growing complexity of transactions in day-to-day working. There is more information to manage just to keep up.

Management theorists focus on the organization as the cornerstone of the new economy and argue that organizations will have to become capable of faster action, greater flexibility, and innovation. Managing change becomes central to an organization's mission, and that mission can best be carried out by more decentralized, less bureaucratic organizations. Management will be a function carried out by increasing numbers of people in the organization.

The New Workplace

The new economy is bringing about changes in tasks, roles, and the exercise of authority in the workplace. These changes constitute a fundamental shift in the nature of work itself, with profound implications for the psychology of work life.

Schor (1992) has suggested that, with the increase in managerial and professional work, there has been a steady increase over the past 20 years in the hours worked for the average employed person.[3] This organizational "speed-up" has fostered workers' exchange of leisure for status and material comfort.

Kanter, taking a less jaundiced view of the increased number of hours worked, emphasizes the lure of the work itself in the postentrepreneurial economy. Individuals in organizations are now working in more complex, emotionally involving, and time-consuming situations. The work is more absorbing, challenging, even exciting, as groups of people combine and recombine to undertake urgent new projects. This involvement must achieve a high level of intensity quickly if ad hoc groups are to be able to work together effectively. Less routine tasks, more fluid roles, and more diffuse authority encourage more personal and informal relationships. That men and women are now more likely to work together in teams, often for long hours, makes the work all the more compelling. As Kanter has observed, an intense love affair with one's work can easily lead to an intense love affair with one's coworker. Sexual excitement and romance, once taboo in the workplace, are now more accepted and out in the open.

Hirschhorn (1988; 1996, personal communication) has likewise observed that in the new economy tasks are less mechanical and work is no longer as reducible to a set of regular procedures and formulas. As work becomes more situational and less routine, people must integrate an increasingly diverse set of facts, interests, and claims.

At the heart of Hirschhorn's argument is the idea that these changes in task are linked to a different experience of boundaries in the workplace. In the bureaucratic organization, boundaries are fixed by rules. People work with relatively clear distinctions among departments and divisions, between the organization and its customers. In the postindustrial milieu, people outside a particular department, division, or organization are more

---

3. Schor calculates that from 1948 to 1987 the average employed person was on the job an additional 163 hours per year. For men, the increase was 98 hours, whereas for women it was 305 hours.

psychologically present. It is more difficult for people in one unit to deny the claims and experiences of people in another unit. Thus, boundaries are more permeable; they are more subject to negotiation and definition in relation to a particular task.

Similarly, authority relationships are less contained in fixed roles and structures and are more subject to negotiation (Hirschhorn, 1996, personal communication). Indeed, the shift from a workplace characterized by fixed "command and control" structures to one based on more contingent, matrixed or networked authority is a defining characteristic of the new workplace. Work is increasingly carried out by teams, the composition of which changes from project to project. Authority shifts as leaders are assigned or emerge *for a particular project*. Reporting relationships become more complex; having one boss becomes the exception rather than the rule.

In the postindustrial workplace, status and rank become encumbrances rather than the bedrock of organizational life. Drucker (1993) has postulated that the role of manager has been redefined from "someone who is responsible for the performance of people" to "someone who is responsible for the application and performance of knowledge" (p. 44). As the need to disseminate, integrate, and apply information outweighs the importance of "command and control," knowledge specialists or associates replace subordinates. Drucker believes that the new organization must be based on shared responsibility:

> [I]n the knowledge-based organization all members have to be able to control their own work by feedback from the results to their objectives. All members must ask themselves: "What is the one *major* contribution to this organization and its mission which I can make at this particular time?" It requires, in other words, that all members act as responsible decision makers. . . . Next it is the responsibility of all members to communicate their objectives, their priorities, and their intended contributions to their fellow workers—up, down, and sideways. And it is the responsibility of all members to make sure that their own objectives fit in with the objectives of the entire group [p. 108].

The New Career

The emergence over the past 25 years of a new economy coupled with the decline of labor unions has significantly affected the employer–employee contract. As organizations have become more committed to the flexibility and innovation needed to manage change, they have become less committed to individual employees. Increasingly, organizations operate with a relatively smaller but highly skilled core of employees; employees are added and subtracted as projects and large-scale initiatives change. Employers have insisted on, and have largely won, the right to shed workers and rehire as circumstances dictate. Thus, there has been a marked increase in "contracting out" and in part-time and temporary employment.[4] Indeed, all jobs have become more contingent in nature (Kanter, 1989; Axmith, 1997).

As one labor economist has put it "If the workplace is a family, our economy is full of broken homes" (Doolittle, 1996, personal communication). In keeping with the weakening of authority structures in organizational life, there has been a change in the overall employment contract, with less commitment from the employer side and less loyalty from the employee side. Kanter (1989) has stated emphatically that loyalty must no longer be to the company but to the self. The accruing of "organizational capital" that historically came from long tenure and an ascending position in a particular company has lost much of its value.[5] The burden is now on the individual to demonstrate a ready understanding of and fit with an organization's structure, functions, and culture. He must continuously prove his value on a project-by-project basis. At the same time, he does well to keep his options open, maintaining strong external networks.

With employment less secure, careers are characterized by more risk and volatility. Job hopping has replaced ladder climbing as the best metaphor for how careers in organizations progress. Managers as well as technicians are more likely to see their skills as portable rather than as tied to a particular organization. As merit pay and bonuses tied to special projects alternate with the periods of unemployment tied to job hopping, there is more variation in wages from year to year (*New York Times*, August 18, 1996).

Kanter (1989) has described the changing nature of careers in the new economy as the shift from "corpocratic" to a blending of professional and entrepreneurial careers *within* organizations. In the traditional corpocratic career, strong attachments to the organization and weak attachments to the task or work group are encouraged. Position in the organizational hier-

---

4. The increase in temporary employment *at all levels of the workforce* has been dramatic—from 619,000 nationally in 1983 to 2.25 million in 1994 (*New York Times*, May 20, 1996)

5. Change in the overall employment contract has been manifested in a shift in compensation generally away from position-based pay toward merit pay and bonuses (Kanter, 1989, *New York Times*, February 25, 1996).

archy is the defining characteristic of career. When the corpocratic gives way to the more professional career structure, reputation becomes the defining characteristic of career. In this model of career, the individual seeks to enhance her reputation (both inside and outside the organization) by taking on increasingly demanding and challenging tasks. The blending of professional with entrepreneurial characteristics in the new model of career means that the individual requires the freedom, independence, and control (traditionally associated with entrepreneurship) to undertake and carry out the projects that increase skills and build reputation. Kanter concludes:

> Like it or not, more and more people will find their careers shaped by how they develop and market their skills and their ideas—and not by the sequence of jobs provided by one corporation. More people will be in and out of business for themselves at more points in their careers, as they enter and leave corporations, as they start and grow businesses, as they combine with peers to offer professional services for still other businesses and corporations. Some postentrepreneurial careers will still unfold within the embrace of a large corporation, but they will be marked less by promotions to greater administrative responsibility and more by project opportunities blending professional skills and innovative ideas. Overall, the power of the position is giving way to the power of the person. A formal title and its placement on an organization chart have less to do with career prospects and career success in a post-entrepreneurial world than the skills and ideas a person brings to that work [pp. 318–319].

The Changing Psychology of Work life

The new economy has led to changes in the workplace and in the very nature of career that are influencing the psychological parameters of work life. These effects are exerted over time and constitute a complex, changing set of conditions that people adapt and respond to in a variety of ways. No two persons are affected the same way.

Overall, changes in the workplace and career interdigitate with the increasing prominence in our society of narcissistic elements of the personality (Lasch, 1978; Kohut, 1984). I do not mean this in a pejorative sense, for I believe that, at least for a significant portion of the workforce, these changes create real opportunities for personality growth and development. The important thing is to "locate" the broader forces that are driving change in *each individual's work life* so as best to facilitate effective responses to them.

Some theorists and researchers (Kanter, 1989; Hochschild, 1997) have suggested that, with the increased time spent at work and the less formal, more fluid relationships that are becoming characteristic of organizations, the postindustrial workplace is increasingly becoming a center of social life. But if, as Hochschild believes, our society's relational center of gravity is shifting to the workplace, as clinicians we should look further at the models of relationship that are emerging.

Relationships in the new workplace are both compelling and inherently limited. Although modern team relationships allow for more expressive needs than in the past, they are still, at bottom, instrumental in nature. As important as the relationships are among team members, as important as the process elements of the group are, the goal remains primary. While work groups are more personal in nature than ever before, they are still defined by the parameters of role and task. Thus, the personal risks involved and the degree of intimacy achieved, though greater than in the past, are circumscribed. I believe that it is the ways in which role and task shield the personality in workplace relationships and provide a degree of safety that makes these relationships so appealing.

In the past, when the composition of a department was more fixed, conflicts and transferences built over time either had to be resolved or lived with. These conditions support the growth of psychic structure. More than ever before, however, work relationships tend to be short term. The fluidity of matrix reporting and project groups and the increased tendency of individuals to maintain a view outside the organization mean that relationships lack a certain gravity and permanence. In the ad hoc, matrixed workplace of today, problematic relationships assume greater saliency in the short term and less importance over the long term.

Relationships in the new workplace are becoming increasingly personal, urgent, and exciting while at the same time more short term and fluid. The feelings of being needed and the sense of recognition that can be derived from workplace relationships are very compelling, but still instrumental in nature. While there is more openness and sharing of the personality than in traditional, hierarchical organizations, these relationships are still relatively low risk compared with intimate romantic and family relationships. It is the excitement of these relationships combined with their relative ease and safety that should raise a clinician's concern. To the extent that instrumental relatedness is mistaken for intimacy and part-object relating taken for whole-object relating, the interpersonal milieu of the new workplace can prevent growth beyond the narcissistic level of object relations.

Hirschhorn (1988), describing the postindustrial milieu, has focused on important changes in the typical anxieties and defenses of work life. In the industrial milieu, relatively fixed boundaries among units and departments of an organization and between the organization and the external world reinforced the defenses of splitting and projection. Anxiety could be reduced by means of the unconscious scenario, "Our work group [department, organization, section] is good; the problems lie in the other work group [department, organization] we must unfortunately depend on." Hirschhorn has pointed out that, in the postindustrial milieu, individuals increasingly work at the boundaries of systems. Working at the boundaries in and of itself creates anxiety because there is less opportunity for splitting and projection. The needs, claims, and experiences of those across the boundary can no longer be denied. Instead, a delicate psychological balancing act goes on in which the needs and claims of "outsiders" need to be ever more completely understood without overwhelming the ability of "insiders" to accomplish their tasks.

There are potential benefits for individual psychological development in the postindustrial milieu described by Hirschhorn. If the anxiety of working at the boundary can be tolerated, movement along a gradient from splitting and projection to empathy, identification and higher level defenses is encouraged. The continuous process of assessing and defining the proper boundary at work is analogous to the progressive definition of body boundaries in individual development, which becomes a cornerstone of identity. Successful work at the boundary leads to a more integrated and holistic understanding of the organization and of how one's own efforts fit into it. Increased demands on the synthetic and integrative functions of the ego, if they are not overwhelming in nature, can effectively further individual psychological development.

The flattening of hierarchy and a decreased emphasis on command and control authority have already been noted as distinguishing characteristics of the new workplace. Hirschhorn (1996, personal communication) has noted that there is more vulnerability on either side of the authority pair in the postindustrial milieu compared with traditional hierarchical organizations. The leader, now more dependent than before on her followers, more openly acknowledges her limitations as part of the influencing process. Followers now move in and out of project leadership positions themselves and take more overall responsibility for their jobs. Thus, authority is more of a negotiation in the postindustrial milieu, based on knowledge as well as communication and influencing skills.

Hirschhorn has stated that hierarchical authority structures gave rise to infantile transferences that, in turn, helped to sustain these structures. With the decline of the traditional organization, these transferences have become major obstacles to the functioning of the work group. There is a potential synergy here that entails decreased infantile transferences to authority, increased productivity, and more opportunities for individual authenticity and self-expression.

Theorists of the new economy agree that both work and career will increasingly entail more risk. The loosening of the employment bond means less security for workers at all levels of the organization, from line workers who are laid off when production needs change to seven-figure CEOs who are fired if they fail to turn a company around rapidly. The postindustrial workplace is becoming less family-like in the conventional sense of providing stability and security in a rapidly changing world. Dependency needs are less likely to be gratified, and individual initiative becomes more critical.

Kanter (1989) has proposed that career security be redefined as emanating not from the organization but from within the individual. She has suggested that in the postentrepreneurial economy security comes not from being employed but from being employable. The organization gives the individual the opportunity to learn and use new skills, which will supposedly make him more employable. Organizations become attractive to the individual to the extent that they provide learning opportunities that will provide long-term employability. But Kanter's point is that even the best organizations will provide these opportunities without the promise of long-term job stability. Careers will become increasingly portable, with the responsibility falling on the individual to be flexible and energetic enough to pursue opportunities to develop the skills that will make him employable.

Kanter's idea of employability security calls into question not only traditional concepts of job security, but also basic ideas of what makes people productive at work. Historically, it has been thought that people are most productive when uncertainty about continuing employment is kept to a minimum. Anxiety about potential job loss has been seen as a detriment to productivity. Recently, the terms of the debate have changed. Anxiety and uncertainty have been recast as risk. Risk is unavoidable and needs to be managed as a necessary part of a career. The implied psychological bargain in the new workplace is a reduction in security for a potential increase in challenge, excitement, and a feeling of being important. The worker trades a sense of being important derived from a long-term commitment by the employer for a sense of being important in a short-term, project-management sense.

Can the challenge and excitement of the new workplace and the rewards of an increased sense of personal importance and skill development enable people to manage limited employer commitments and a complex job market? Will employees meet these new demands with the initiative and energy that increase productivity while enabling them increasingly to manage their own careers? In short, is there a new model of what makes people productive at work?

I believe the answer is a qualified yes. First, I suggest that there will be marked variability by personality type in how productive people will be in the face of the anxiety, uncertainty, and insecurity of the new economy. As clinicians, we know that people vary greatly in the extent to which they require external structure to feel secure and be productive. Those with relatively high needs for externally given security will increasingly require remediation and counseling to become self-managing in the career sense. Second, increased stress will be an inevitable by-product of the insecurity of the new workplace, even if there is a positive response in productivity. The stress may be manifested in increased workers' compensation and disability claims and other kinds of workplace incidents. Third, a new model of productivity hinges on the workplace's becoming a true learning culture. While challenge, excitement, and a heightened sense of personal importance are very real "high arousal" motivators, consistent opportunities for learning and the development of skills will provide critical "moderate arousal" motivators. I believe that the need for learning throughout the life cycle has been inadequately recognized and provided for in our society. If the new workplace can provide real, plentiful, good-faith opportunities for transferable learning and skill development, a new employment contract may be forged. These opportunities could so advance the growth and development of the personality that people may be able to cope with less job security.

WINNERS AND LOSERS IN A CHANGING WORKPLACE

Changes in the tasks, roles, and organizational structures of the postindustrial economy over time affect the shape and composition of the workforce. Particular qualifications, skills, and, I believe, personality characteristics are more sought after whereas others seem poorly adapted to the new workplace. Thus, the relative value (in labor/economic terms) of identifiable groups undergoes change, sometimes dramatic, sometimes barely perceptible. I have suggested that organizations are increasingly reward-ing individuals who take initiative, accept risk, are flexible and nonhier-archically oriented, and have good communication and team-building skills. The capacity to reinvent oneself and one's own career, to view the self rather than the profession or the organization as the locus of career definition, is also part of the picture. Cautious, security-oriented, rigidly bounded, per-fectionistic personalities like the compulsive are less well-adapted to the new workplace than they were to the traditional organization.

The new economy requires a highly educated, technically proficient workforce. Drucker (1993) argues that the greatest employment need of the next decades will be for "technicians" in the broadest sense, those highly skilled workers who have formal knowledge, formal education, and a capacity for formal learning. Drucker believes that, with such workers in relatively short supply, organizations will increasingly focus resources on attracting higher level "knowledge workers," holding on to them, and recognizing and rewarding them. A crude measure of this emerging real-ity is already evident in the increasing "premium" wage for college-educated workers. Although wages were stagnant for the workforce overall from 1979 to 1995, they exploded for college-educated men during the same period—from 40% more than high school graduates to 75% more (*New York Times*, October 15, 1995).[6]

Those who are educated and technically proficient and have personal-ity types characterized by initiative, flexibility, interactiveness, and infor-mality are likely to be winners in the new economy. But what will happen to those who have been more marginal players in traditional organizations, such as women and the unskilled? How will family life be affected by the very compelling demands of the new workplace?

Work and Gender

The evolution of a knowledge-based economy has coincided with a seis-mic shift in the gender distribution of the workforce. According to the *New York Times* (October 9, 1994), women as a proportion of the work-force increased from 44.7% in 1973 to 57.9% in 1993. From 1979 to 1995, women's wages overall increased 7.6% while men's *decreased* 9% (*New York Times*, February 25, 1996). For men aged 25 to 34, real wages decreased by 25% from 1973 to 1993 (*New York Times*, October 15, 1995). Although

---

6. That the premium increased so dramatically for men and not for women is very significant and is further discussed in the section on gender and the workforce.

the ranks of senior management are still overwhelmingly male, some believe that, overall, women's wages have almost achieved parity with men's when the effects of absence from the workforce related to child-rearing are factored in (Crittenden, 1995).

I believe that the relationship between the emerging knowledge-based economy and the dramatic increase in women (and women's wages) in the workforce is far from accidental. Remember Drucker's (1993) estimate that jobs "making and moving things," still a majority in the 1950s, had decreased to 20% of the workforce by 1990. These were jobs in which brute force was an asset, making them better suited, for the most part, to men. As production work has decreased and changed to require more skill, men's wages have declined. Women's wages, which were much less tied to production work, have been less affected. Another way of looking at this change is that there has been a marked decrease in lower level jobs historically associated with men (production, transportation, laborer), but an increase in lower level jobs usually associated with women (clerical, sales, and service) (*New York Times*, December 1, 1994). Wages have shifted commensurately.

Burtless (1990), analyzing trends in the labor force through the late 1980s, has provided a more nuanced picture of these developments. He showed that wage inequality was on the rise for men but was falling or fairly stable for women. Wage differentials had increased for men in the 80s because of increased demand for skilled workers across industries, the decline in labor unions, and the relative scarcity of college-educated young men. The marked decrease in goods-producing jobs requiring little skill deprived men of an important source of moderately paid jobs and left a surplus of unskilled male workers in a labor market requiring more skill and education than ever.

With less educated men being effectively pushed out of the new economy, there has been an overall change in the pattern of male employment. From the 1970s to the 1980s the percentage of men aged 22 to 58 working full-time, year-round in eight of ten years decreased from 80% to 70%. For black men, the percentage working full-time decreased from 75% to 50% during the same period!

I believe that the shift in gender distribution of the workforce has created stress and opportunity for both men and women. Let us view these psychological effects through the lens of the vital, yet conflicted relationship each sex has with work.

I have previously (Axelrod, 1994, 1995) discussed the work of several authors regarding the critical relationship between male self-esteem and work. Greenson (1968) emphasized the fragility of male gender identity by pointing out that the separation-individuation process requires the little boy not only to move away from psychic unity with the mother but, at the same time, to shift from a primary identification with the mother toward one with the father. This shift in identification leaves the pull toward symbiotic merger with the mother a lifelong threat to the male's ego intactness and gender identity. Aggression-dominated counteridentifications with mother, and with women generally, can be brought into play to "prop up" the sense of maleness. Optimally, though, a gendered ego ideal emerges in early childhood that leads a boy toward a secure sense of maleness. The male ego ideal has its origins in the turn away from the mother toward action and mastery in the external world, colored by inborn capacities for aggression, large-motor activity, and relational disjunction rather than attunement (W. Olesker, 1995, personal communication). Eventually, work life becomes an important component of the male ego ideal, with important consequences for men's relationship to their work.

Gilmore (1990), in his cross-cultural study of masculinity, observed that most societies make the distinction between biological maturation and "real manhood." The latter needs dramatic proof and must be won against powerful odds. Most societies evolve a combination of tests that must be passed and ideals that must be espoused for "true manhood" to be identified. I have argued (Axelrod, 1995) that the expenditure of significant physical or mental energy (or both) in overcoming environmental challenges to gain success at work becomes an important ritual or marker of "true manhood" in many cultures. Men's relationship to their work can be colored by deeply rooted needs to "pass the test" and prove their manhood. Additionally, the intensity of men's relationship to their work may draw on deep needs for creative self-expression that they cannot experience in pregnancy and childbirth.

I believe that there was an implicit psychological contract between men and work in industrial society that has left men psychologically vulnerable in the postindustrial society. An economy based on "making and moving things" fit with male superiority in size and strength and gave men an advantage in the workforce. Modes of command and control dominated modern industrial society, even when not specifically applied to goods production. These modes of relating to work and to others in the workplace fit well with more tangible and concrete aspects of the male ego ideal. They were broadly accessible to men, educated or not.

The postindustrial economy's shift away from making and moving things and from the associated modes of command and control has left men psychologically vulnerable on a number of scores. As the demand for specifically male labor has decreased, the sense of secure manhood that derives from earning a livelihood and providing for others has become more tenuous. Men at the bottom rungs of the economy have been particularly hard hit in this regard. Lacking in education and skills, they have nowhere to go in the new economy, and their wages and continuity of employment have suffered accordingly. A sense of impotence has been expressed in feelings of confusion and anger, some of it directed toward women.

But it is not only unskilled men who are more vulnerable in the postindustrial economy. The conventional, gender-segregated workplace served important functions for the male psyche and bound anxiety in significant ways. The "male workplace" not only gave men the chance to compete and prove their manhood, it strengthened male social bonds, providing opportunities for sublimated expression of threatening homosexual feelings. The gender-segregated workplace gave men a sphere of activity removed from women. As such, it strengthened male defenses against the anxiety of "reabsorption" into the orbit of women, although these defenses were primarily those of splitting and projection.

What are men's prospects in the changing workplace? First and foremost, the outcome will hinge on their capacity for learning. In childhood, male difficulties with modulation of anger, control of impulses, and focusing of attention contribute to a high incidence of learning disabilities compared with females. The adult residues of these learning difficulties will become increasingly costly to male economic survival. Furthermore, to the extent that there is a male cognitive style consisting of a tendency to focus single-mindedly on a task, it will have to be mitigated by the ability to attend to multiple sources of information embedded in a matrix.

Second, men may experience increased anxiety as gender-based splitting and projection become less adaptive in the gender-integrated workplace. Men will have to work through feelings of loss, anger, and resentment toward women that accompany their change in status. As the workplace becomes increasingly gender integrated, men will have to deal simultaneously with the distracting effects of sexual attraction and derivatives of primal wishes to be taken care of as well as fears of reabsorption into the maternal orbit. Men's experiences of being threatened in both regards can contribute to the regressive behavior (e.g., harassment and discrimination) that threatens their effectiveness.

Third, characteristic male forms of self-expression in work will not entirely disappear but will continue to affect the postindustrial workplace. Male tendencies toward command and control, as well as single-minded focus, will continue to be evident, and sometimes adaptive, in the new workplace. In the new economy, men will have fewer opportunities to prove their manhood through brute force or through counteridentifications with women. Yet opportunities will continue to exist for men to test their mettle through feats of endurance and mental strength. Manhood rituals may shape the culture of specific units or departments of organizations, where bragging about the superhuman pace and long hours as well as salary and bonus levels become an important part of social interaction. Careful distinctions will no doubt have to be made between the legitimate male needs to bond and compete through work and the creation of a distinctly "female unfriendly" atmosphere.

In turning to the implications of the changing workplace for women, I again emphasize the fact that knowledge work, which requires a high level of skill and education, is essentially gender neutral. The increased demand for knowledge workers has leveled the playing field when it comes to gender participation in the workforce. Not only are women not at a disadvantage in this kind of work, there may be a particularly good fit between women and the new workplace.

I believe that, compared with the workplace of the postwar era, there is a relatively good synchrony between the current workplace and women's ways of knowing and experiencing, partly because of the decreased relevance of gender dimorphism as the trend is away from making and moving things. This synchrony also derives from decreased emphasis on hierarchy and command and control authority in organizations. Instead, the new workplace is built on matrix management, team work, and an extremely high volume of information sharing. The new workplace puts a premium on forms of interaction and communication akin to those at which women have traditionally excelled. For example, Tannen (1995) has observed that girls and women are more likely to get things done by giving suggestions rather than giving orders and are more likely than men to do things for the good of the group. Their conversational rituals are more egalitarian than hierarchical as they, more than men, try to restore balance to a conversation and take into account the effect of their words on others.

Rosener (1992) has suggested that women's ways of leading may be particularly well suited to a workforce that increasingly demands participation. She found that women in organizations tend to use "interactive leadership," characterized by encouraging participation, sharing power and information, enhancing the self-worth of others, and energizing others. Interactive leadership is in marked contrast to the command and control leadership that has been associated with men and is less well adapted to the new workplace.

Women's experience in the new workplace is, however, typically more complicated than the version depicted by Rosener. Not only do women have to deal with male discrimination, harassment, and reluctance to give up power, they also have to sort out the complex links between work and self-esteem.

In one of the few psychoanalytic articles on women and work, Applegarth (1976) observed that women as a group have low self-esteem and doubt their capacities. Strong feelings of inferiority color women's relationships to their work. For many women, work life is valued precisely because it provides an important means of demonstrating competence in the external world and disproving an inner sense of inferiority. For neurotic women, whose feelings of low self-esteem are refractory to actual accomplishments, the workplace, especially interactions with men, can become highly charged and distressing. For better integrated women, conflict can still be intense between the aggression that is an integral part of successful working and leading and their sense of femininity (Nadelson, 1990). Even as images of femininity change and new models of leadership evolve that seem better suited to women (e.g., "interactive leadership"), women can still be plagued by a deep-seated fear that success at work is unfeminine. This conflict can lead some women to downplay their very real accomplishments or to use male styles of performance as a standard for self-evaluation.

Conflicts experienced between success at work and a sense of femininity can intensify during the years of childbirth and child rearing. The needs to express aggression through work and leadership can be felt as inimical to the need to protect children from aggression and danger in the outside world. This aspect of women's conflict between aggression and femininity is an important factor that fuels their sometimes consuming concerns with balancing work and family.

Balancing Work and Family

With the surge of women into the workforce, the sharp increase in two- or more job families, and the greater prevalence of female-headed households, difficulties in balancing the demands of work and family have come to the forefront of the national consciousness. Juliet Schor (1992) has shown that parents' available time for children has decreased 10 hours per week from 1960 to 1986. Coping with this time squeeze has included attempts at increased household efficiency—the "outsourcing" of children's activities (Hochschild, 1997), the emphasis on "quality time" with children, and the like. Still, the guilt felt by parents, especially mothers, is enormous. As Hochschild has suggested, this guilt may be a kind of "reality check" on the fact that raising children is a time-intensive enterprise that does not readily accommodate itself to the requirements of the workplace. The demands of work and family seem to be on a collision course, and, while all family members pay a price, it is women who are daily most preoccupied with the conflict.

Arlie Hochschild (1997) has outlined a highly perceptive analysis of today's work–family conflict. Using a major corporation as a case study, she observed that very few people were taking advantage of the company's progressive "family friendly" policies. Since increased use of leave time and part-time work seem to offer a way out of the "time bind," Hochschild wondered why they were not being used more. She considered the possibility that women feel that these family-friendly policies are mere window dressing and that using them would inevitably penalize the employee. While this perception of family-friendly policies may play a part, she came to the startling conclusion that men and women are spending more time at work because they simply find it more pleasurable than being at home.

Hochschild's conclusion, disconcerting as it is, is based on a reading of the psychology of the new workplace similar to the ideas developed earlier in this chapter. She showed that the emphasis on teamwork and communal problem solving in the new workplace gives people a sense of being important to each other that has made the workplace, rather than the family or community, the center of social life. At work people depend on each other and trust each other, but in a way that is much more manageable than in the intimate sphere of home life. Relationships are rewarding, in large part, *because* they are circumscribed and controlled. They are not subject to the regressive pull of intimate relationships at home, with all the chaos and urgency of young children's needs.

Hochschild has grasped the fact that the new workplace is built on a gratifying cycle of challenge, mastery, and feelings of importance and appreciation. By contrast, not only is family life with children less predictable, but positive feedback and personal recognition are neither as immediate nor as reliable. Mom may have an important job in the organization, but at home she is just Mom and as such is inevitably subject to her children's needs, frustrations, and angers as well as their appreciation. Hochschild understands that we are infinitely more vulnerable at home because it is our capacity to love and to forge, deepen, and repair intimate relationships that is the determining factor.

Hochschild believes that growing numbers of women seem reluctant to spend the time at home that child rearing requires. The pull of the workplace is very powerful, with its well-defined sense of competence, importance, and appreciation compared with the free-floating feelings of guilt and inadequacy at home. The danger, as Hochschild sees it, is that the seductive appeal of managed relationships in the workplace will win out over the riskier relationships of the family, with potentially serious consequences for children's emotional development. Faced with the need to reach deep inside emotionally to make family relationships work, women, at least in the corporation Hochschild studied, seem to be opting for the relative safety of the workplace. Hochschild concludes that this psychological dynamic is a major barrier to more concrete, problem-solving approaches to the problem of work–family balance and needs to be given more consideration by policy makers.

Hochschild focused on the plight of women because the mother "still represents the heart and soul, warmth and kindness of family life" (p. 233). But if women are preoccupied with and conflicted by the demands of work and family, might men not be able to play a critical role in resolving the problem of work–family balance? Certainly, this has been the hope of many theorists and researchers. Hochschild (1989), showed that although women were doing a disproportionate share of work in the home, in some cases men were sharing the burden more or less equally. It was her hope, and the hope of many, that this trend would increase. Yet, by the time Hochschild (1997) wrote *The Time Bind* less than 10 years later, this option was little more than a footnote to her main argument. What had happened?

Although there is some evidence that a small amount of change has taken place in the gender distribution of housework and child care, Hochschild has observed that "outsourcing" is a more likely solution to the child care and housework demands than is a true redistribution of effort by gender. In her more recent book there is an implicit tone of resignation to the still relatively limited role of men in the day-to-day functioning of the family. Her focus is on what she sees as the disturbing new trend of women joining men in their flight from the family to the workplace.

To my knowledge, neither Hochschild nor anyone else has paid much attention to the psychological underpinnings of men's resistance to changing the balance between work and family. I have tried to show that the relationship between male self-esteem and work is deeply rooted and not easily modified. Especially during early adulthood a man's need to prove his worth through work cannot be taken lightly (Axelrod, 1997). Phallic strivings, characterized by single-minded focus, task orientation, and tests of endurance gain expression through work life. If men feel these needs are being compromised by increased attention to home life, they are apt to resist a gender redistribution of housework and child care.

I am not suggesting that *all* men are incapable of a more equal work–family arrangement with their partners. Certainly there are men who are temperamentally suited to such arrangements. Often older, remarried men establishing second families, who have already proved themselves in the workplace, are particularly good candidates for such sharing. However, the more diffuse attention, permeable boundaries, and noninstrumental orientation that seem essential to successful child rearing do not come easily to many men. There is a strong pull toward spending "down time" alone rather than providing for the expressive needs of family members.

Male resistance to more equal work–family relationships may be exacerbated by a fear of being feminized. The pull toward the interior life of the family may be deeply anxiety provoking for men who have not resolved their fears of reabsorption into the world of women. I believe there are more of such men than theorists and policy makers would like to believe. For many men, the key to shifting focus to the "inside" of family life will continue to be the quality of the relationship with their partners and the nature of their intimate dialogue. The ability of a man and a woman to resolve the problem of work–family balance hinges on their capacity for true intimacy based on both acceptance of and true enjoyment of sexual difference. To the extent that insecurity, envy, and resentment color the marital relationship, it will be difficult to strike a balance between the "outside" of the workplace and the "inside" of the home. All too often the challenge of balancing work and family can become a battleground dominated by the unresolved emotional needs and gender identity issues of the partners.

Welfare to Work

The work–family dilemma is particularly difficult for welfare recipients and has become even more acute with increasing work requirements. This segment of the population, largely unskilled, poorly educated, and often inexperienced in work, would face major obstacles to employment even without the complications of young children and broken relationships.

Given the relative absence of stable marriage and partnership bonds among these young lower socioeconomic status adults, they are often very much alone in facing the demands of the workplace. Although social programs have been designed to help welfare recipients (especially women) make the transition from welfare to work, their success has been limited. I believe that with a few exceptions (e.g., Project Match, described further later) psychological barriers to the transition from welfare to work have not been adequately considered. In this section of the chapter, I offer a clinical perspective on the welfare to work transition.

William Julius Wilson (1997) has most eloquently linked the growth of the "underclass" and its symptomatology to the decline in production work for unskilled, poorly educated minority men in the inner cities. Entry-level jobs making and moving things were highly structured and structuring in the psychological sense. They were thus relatively accessible psychologically to young minority men. The disappearance of many of these jobs affects a community because over time a lack of employment opportunity in disadvantaged segments of society becomes woven into the "group psyche" as chronic depression, psychological fragility, and a vulnerability to stress.

The irreversibility of the economic, social, and psychological trends of the past 30 years means that there is probably no simple jobs policy that will put poor, minority families and communities back together again. With the dearth of well-paying unskilled jobs in the new economy, more comprehensive preparation will be required for more psychologically demanding work. Nor will it be realistic to focus primarily on young men, as the gender distribution of the workforce has shifted.

The needs of young men and women at the bottom rungs of the economy seem to have diverged considerably, and preemployment programs are typically sex segregated. The men are frequently unattached and are receiving job-related assistance as part of drug rehabilitation, criminal justice, or family court systems. The emphasis in employment programs for men is often on relapse prevention and responsible fatherhood (especially the need to make child-support payments) as well as on job-related skills. For women with young children on public assistance, complex practical and emotional issues in balancing work and family cannot be separated from the emphasis on job-related skills. Because of the attention that is being focused nationwide on the AFDC program, more information is available on the plight of these young women, and my discussion centers on them.

The psychological obstacles facing welfare women's movement into the job market are considerable. According to one study, 42% of the women in a welfare-to-work program had symptoms of clinical depression, twice the percentage in the general population (*New York Times*, February 27, 1996). In many cases, the treatment of depression, anxiety-related disorders, and other forms of psychopathology may be a prerequisite for effective welfare-to-work interventions. With the recent passage of welfare time limits and universal work requirements, however, the emphasis in social policy has been away from treatment-oriented, indeed educationally oriented, preparation for work. The current ideology is that treatment and education have limited transferability to the world of work, that the best preparation for work is work or work-related activity itself. Thus, I believe, for this population, therapeutic issues will increasingly come up not as a prelude to work, but in the actual context of work life.

I believe that as clinicians observing the debates on welfare, we have been reluctant to point out the therapeutic effects of work itself. Because the new welfare requirements seemed designed to herd a reluctant workforce into distasteful, low-paying jobs, their beneficial effects on the welfare clients themselves was initially the domain of political conservatives only. However, the potential of the work requirements to energize a sizable segment of the welfare client group became apparent soon after the law's passage. The activity of working and the payoffs in terms of increased self-esteem and feelings of efficacy in and of themselves have potent effects in combating the depression that is pervasive in welfare recipients. The beneficial effects of work requirements are consistent with what we as clinicians should know: that withdrawal and inactivity are symptoms of depression, and the effective treatment of depression requires, among other things, clear encouragement of activity. Thus, the idea that there is a sequence from treatment of depression to engagement in work activity is, in many cases, inaccurate and oversimplified. The work activity is often an important part of the treatment process, just as the capacity to work may require ongoing treatment.

Effective intervention in the transition from welfare to work requires much more than a clear message supporting the value of work activity. Any successful program must address not only practical issues like child care and transportation, but also the psychological barriers to employment on the part of welfare clients. These barriers include the very strong pull that exclusive child rearing has for these women. The wish for reparenting that accompanies *all* parenting is especially strong among women who have not had reliable sources of love, stability, and self-esteem. Moreover, women from backgrounds with few educational and vocational opportunities develop a kind of cultural agoraphobia that many in the middle class fail to appreciate. The intimate mother–child orbit represents relative safety for women who feel ill equipped and frightened of entering the mainstream culture represented by the workplace.

Work requirements may be effective in moving welfare recipients into some form of work activity but will probably have less influence on the critical issue of job retention. Yet it is not getting a job but keeping a job and moving purposefully to a better one that will make the long-term difference in the plight of the underclass. Intervention to increase job retention is more difficult and requires more psychological sophistication than programs limited to job finding (Herr, Wagner, and Halpern, 1996).

One program with extensive experience in the field of job retention for welfare clients is the Chicago-based Project Match. The program's director, Toby Herr (1997, personal communication), emphasized the long-term counseling perspective that is essential for success in this area. Welfare recipients typically have difficulty functioning in their first jobs and may need many jobs before they can really retain a job and feel confident of remaining in the workforce. In contrast to most programs that terminate the supportive relationship after the job is found, Project Match provides a consistent, long-term relationship between counselor and client. This relationship continues across episodes of job finding and losing.

Two levels of skill are essential to job retention. The first level entails meeting the requirements for attendance and punctuality. Herr believes that most clients are able to acquire these skills, even if it takes several jobs to do so. The next level of skill is more challenging and takes longer—it pertains to the mastery of the interpersonal and self-management requirements of the job. In contrast to the more routine production jobs of the past, present-day entry-level service jobs are relatively complex and interpersonally demanding. The job requirements of sequencing, decision making, and rather complex, task-oriented interactions are formidable for welfare clients from impoverished backgrounds. Herr et al. (1996) describe the interpersonal demands on these clients as follows:

> When it comes to interacting with supervisors, a person must learn about lines of authority and how hierarchies operate and must also accept the fact that most workplaces are not a democracy. When it comes to co-workers, it is important to understand concepts like teamwork and mutual respect. And when it comes to customers and clients, it usually means accepting the dictum that "the customer is always right." With all three types of relationships, there are ways of interacting that are acceptable and unacceptable and these can differ not only in relation to the specific person but also to the specific setting [p. 49].

Learning the skills to manage the day-to-day upset of working, especially in the absence of a network of experienced job holders in the community, takes time. Learning to cope with and effectively resolve workplace conflicts also require relatively high level interpersonal and communication skills that develop over time.

I believe that the need for programs like Project Match will become more apparent as our society progresses from a short-term emphasis on job finding to the longer term perspective of job retention. These are not therapeutic programs per se but are clinically informed programs geared to work life. The long-term relationship between client and counselor, in which personal problems affecting the job can be discussed and interpersonal learning can occur, will be essential. This kind of job coach–client relationship requires a psychologically informed staff, a relatively long-term relationship, and one that is separate from the workplace and endures even as jobs are gained and lost. From a clinical perspective, this seems like an essential ingredient for success in the transition from welfare to work.

THE CLINICIAN AND THE CHANGING WORKPLACE

Why should psychoanalysts concern themselves with the changes in the workplace that have been outlined in this chapter? Broadly speaking, for two reasons. First, as consultants, we have a unique perspective on the impact of these changes on individuals and groups. This perspective has typically been missing from debate and policy initiatives to the detriment of each. In the previous section, on "Winners and Losers in a Changing Workplace," I attempted to bring a clinical psychoanalytic frame of understanding to some important developments in our culture. I believe that further efforts along these lines[7] could enhance the public's understanding of these workplace changes and some of the tensions and resistances associated with them. More effective programs, better attuned to clinical realities, could result.

---

7. For example, psychoanalysts are particularly qualified to address current issues in leadership, especially the vicissitudes of teaching and training leaders. This is too often done in prepackaged seminars that do not take into consideration individual personality style and dynamics. Achieving leadership is one of life's major developmental challenges, and is best facilitated if the *total* personality (including conflicts and developmental dynamics) is taken into consideration.

Second, I believe that understanding changes in the workplace is essential to effective intervention in our patients' work lives. Just as our patients are driven by unconscious psychic forces, so are they influenced by changes in the workplace that are not fully articulated or known. It can be helpful for the therapist to make these broader workplace forces explicit to the patient, as doing so can increase his understanding of his situation and possibly enhance his efficacy.

Broader forces and trends in the workplace can provide both opportunities and obstacles with regard to a patient's treatment goals. A profession's norms and values may change over the course of a patient's career, requiring significant adjustments that parallel changes the patient hopes to make in treatment. For example, William L (chapter 8) had entered a "gentleman's profession" only to find that success depended increasingly on marketing and entrepreneurship. His tendencies toward withdrawal and intellectualization thus became a focus of attention in his work life as well as his personal life. He eventually learned that he could be quite adept at business development but needed to monitor in treatment his tendencies to slip back into a more passive, introverted approach to both work and social relationships. Charles G (chapters 4 and 7) had felt inadequate in his field because his technical skills were not as strong as those of some of his colleagues. Over the course of treatment, however, it became clear that his "people skills," developed in the crucible of a dysfunctional family, were increasingly in demand in a field that was struggling to integrate teamwork with technical know-how. Appreciation of the value of "people skills" in the patient's workplace dovetailed with the therapist's support for the patient's capacities to communicate and influence people, which he had underestimated.

Changes in the workplace may sometimes seem to be at cross-purposes with the goals of treatment and may need to be acknowledged by the therapist. Patients who have had unstable or traumatic childhoods may be ill equipped to cope with the insecurity and fluidity of the current workplace. Being fired or "downsized" may be exactly what these patients *don't* need. The therapist, angry herself at the "realities," nonetheless has to help the patient come to grips with this retraumatization. In contrast, there are patients who are being favorably recognized at work for traits that more broadly interfere with personality growth. For example, Kate R (chapter 8) was being handsomely rewarded at work for her charming, easy-to-get-along with personality. In her case, however, this acceptance reinforced her feelings of emptiness, of accommodating others at the expense of knowing what she wanted. Workaholics, in particular, are likely to be rewarded for compulsive behavior that directly interferes with the development of intimate relationships. (This is the point made more broadly by Hochschild, 1997.) The therapist does well to acknowledge the strength of the forces acting on the patient while helping him learn to tolerate some of the ambiguity, frustration, and lack of control that are an inherent part of the personal realm.

I am suggesting, then, that as clinicians we can be most effective with our patients if we are cognizant of the dynamics of change in the workplace. The evolving workplace makes psychological demands on our patients, more on some than on others, and different according to role and personality structure. In the more dramatic cases (downsizing, sexual harassment) we are called on to do psychological damage control. More typically, we need to understand as much as possible how the requirements of the workplace for changing skills, values, styles of communication and leadership and the like affect our individual patients uniquely. These workplace changes are a critical part of the psychological field within which we strive to facilitate our patients' evolution and growth.

References

Applegarth, A. (1976). Some observations on work inhibitions in women. *Journal of the American Psychoanalytic Association*, 24:251–268.

Auchincloss, E. L. and Michels, R. (1989). The impact of middle age on ambitions and ideals. In J.M. Oldham and R.S. Liebert (Eds.) *The Middle Years: New Psychoanalytic Perspectives*. New Haven, CT: Yale University Press, 1989, pp. 40–57.

Axelrod, S. D. (1994). "Impossible projects": Men's illusory solutions to the problem of work. *Psychoanalytic Psychology*, 11:21–32.

Axelrod, S. D. (1995) Men and work: Aspects of a deep structure of masculinity. Presented at spring meeting Division 39 (Psychoanalysis), American Psychological Association, Santa Monica, CA.

Axelrod, S. D. (1997) The evolution of masculine ideals in adulthood. Presented at spring meeting Division 39 (Psychoanalysis), American Psychological Association, Denver, CO.

Axelrod, S. D. and Axelrod, J. (1987). Staff interaction and therapeutic structure on a short-term psychiatric unit. *Hillside Journal of Clinical Psychiatry*, 9:184–194.

Axmith, M. (1997). The evolving workplace: Its implications for outplacement practice. In A.J. Pickman (Ed.) *Special Challenges in Career Management*. Mahwah, NJ: Lawrence Erlbaum Associates.

Bergmann, M. S. (1987). *The Anatomy of Loving*. New York: Columbia University Press.

Blos, P. (1962). *On Adolescence: A Psychoanalytic Interpretation*. New York: Free Press.

Blos, P. (1985). *Son and Father: Before and Beyond the Oedipus Complex*. New York: Free Presss.

Burtless, G. (Ed.) (1990). *A Future of Lousy Jobs?* Washington, DC: Brookings Institution.

141

Cath, S. H., Gurwitt, A. R., and Ross, J. M. (1982). *Father and Child: Clinical and Developmental Perspectives.* Hillsdale, NJ: The Analytic Press, 1994.

Cath, S. H., Gurwitt, A. R., and Gunsberg, L. (1989). *Fathers and Their Families.* Hillsdale, NJ: The Analytic Press.

Chasseguet-Smirgel, J. (1985). *The Ego Ideal: A Psychoanalytic Essay on the Malady of the Ideal.* New York: Norton.

Colarusso, C. and Nemiroff, R. (1981). *Adult Development.* New York: Plenum.

Crittenden, D. (1995). Yes, motherhood lowers pay. *New York Times* Op-Ed, August 22.

Czander, W. M. (1993). *The Psychodynamics of Work and Organizations.* New York: Guilford.

Drucker, P. (1993). *Post-Capitalist Society.* New York: HarperBusiness.

Erikson, E. (1950). *Childhood and Society.* New York: Norton.

Erikson, E. (1958). *Young Man Luther.* New York: Norton.

Erikson, E. (1968). *Identity: Youth and Crisis.* New York: Norton.

Erikson, E. (1969). *Ghandi's Truth.* New York: Norton.

Fast, I. (1975). Aspects of work style and work difficulty in borderline personalities. *International Journal of Psycho-Analysis,* 56:397–403.

Freud, A. (1965). *Normality and Pathology in Childhood: Assessments of Development.* New York: International Universities Press.

Freud, S. (1916). Some character types met with in psychoanalytic work. *Standard Edition,* 14:309–333. London: Hogarth Press, 1957.

Freud, S. (1930). Civilization and its discontents. *Standard Edition,* 21:59–145. London: Hogarth Press,

Furman, E. (1997). Child's work: Developmental aspects of the capacity to work and enjoy it. In C. W. Socarides and S. Kramer (Eds.) *Work and Its Inhibitions: Psychoanalytic Essays.* Madison, CT: International Universities Press, pp. 3–17.

Gilmore, D. (1990). *Manhood in the Making: Cultural Concepts of Masculinity.* New Haven, CT: Yale University Press.

Gould, R. L. (1972). The phases of adult life: A study in developmental psychology. *American Journal of Psychiatry,* 129:521–531.

Greenson, R. R. (1968). Dis-identifying from mother: Its special importance for the boy. *International Journal of Psychoanalysis,* 49:370–374.

Hartmann, H. (1939). *Ego Psychology and the Problem of Adaptation.* New York: International Universities Press, 1958.

Hendrik, I. (1943). Work and the pleasure principle. *Psychoanalytic Quarterly,* 12:311–329.

Herr, T., Wagner, S. L., and Halpern, R. (1996). *Making the Shoe Fit: Creating a Work-Prep System for a Large and Diverse Welfare Population.* Chicago: Erikson Institute.

Hirschhorn, L. (1990). *The Workplace Within: Psychodynamics of Organizational Life.* Cambridge, MA: MIT Press.

Hochschild, A. (1989). *The Second Shift.* New York: Avon Books.

Hochschild, A. (1997). *The Time Bind: When Work Becomes Home and Home Becomes Work.* New York: Metropolitan Books.

Holmes, D. (1965). A contribution to a psychoanalytic theory of work. *The Psychoanalytic Study of the Child,* 20:384–393. New York: International Universities Press.

Jahoda, M. (1966). Notes on work. In R. Loewenstein (Ed.) *Psychoanalysis: A General Psychology.* New York: International Universities Press, pp. 622–633.

Jaques, E. (1960). Disturbances in the capacity to work. *International Journal of Psychoanalysis,* 41:357–367.

Jaques, E. (1965). Death and the mid-life crisis. In E. Jaques *Creativity and Work.* Madison, CT: International Universities Press, pp. 297–329, 1990.

Kanter, R. M. (1989). *When Giants Learn to Dance.* New York: Touchstone.

Kernberg, O. (1991). Aggression and love in the relationship of the couple. *Journal of the American Psychoanalytic Association,* 39:45–70.

Kets de Vries, M. (1978). Defective adaptation to work. *Bulletin of the Menninger Clinic,* 42:35–50.

Kets de Vries, M. (1983). *The Irrational Executive.* New York: International Universities Press.

Kohut, H. (1971). *The Analysis of the Self.* New York: International Universities Press.

Kohut, H. (1977). *The Restoration of the Self.* New York: International Universities Press.

Kohut, H. (1984). *How Does Analysis Cure?,* A. Goldberg and P. Stepansky (Eds.). Chicago: University of Chicago Press.

Kramer, Y. (1977). Work compulsion: A psychoanalytic study. *Psychoanalytic Quarterly,* 46:361–385.

Lantos, B. (1943). Work and the instincts. *International Journal of Psychoanalysis,* 24:114–119.

Lantos, B. (1952). Metapsychological considerations on the concept of work. *International Journal of Psycho-Analysis,* 33:439–443.

Laplanche, J. and Pontalis, J.-B. (1973). *The Language of Psychoanalysis,* trans. D. Nicholson-Smith. New York: Norton.

Lasch, C. (1978). *The Culture of Narcissism: American Life in an Age of Diminishing Expectations.* New York: Norton.

Lemann, N. (1997). Review of Arlie Hochschild's *The Time Bind* *New York Times Book Review,* May 11.

Levinson, D., Darrow, D., Klein, E., Levinson, M., and Mckee, B. (1978). *The Seasons of a Man's Life.* New York: Ballantine Books.

Medalie, J. (1976). Some dynamics in the development of a commitment to work: A case study. Unpublished manuscript.

Menzies, I. E. P. (1975). A case study in the functioning of social systems as a defense against anxiety. In A. D. Colman and W. H. Bexton (Eds.) *Group Relations Reader.* Sausalito, CA: GREX, pp. 281–312.

Miller, E. J. and Rice, A. K. (1967) *Systems of Organizations*. London: Tavistock.

Modell, A. (1989). Object relations theory: Psychic aliveness in the middle years. In Oldham, J.M. and Liebert, R.S. (Eds.) *The Middle Years: New Psychoanalytic Perspectives*. New Haven: Yale University Press, pp. 17–26.

Nadelson, C. C. (1990). Women leaders: Achievement and power. In R. A. Nemiroff and C. A. Colarusso (Eds.) *New Dimensions in Adult Development*. New York: Basic Books.

Neugarten, B. L. (1968). Adult personality: Toward a psychology of the life cycle. In B. L. Neugarten (Ed.) *Middle Age and Aging*. Chicago: University of Chicago Press.

New York Times (October 9, 1994). Back from the mommy track, section 3, p. 1.

New York Times (December 1, 1994). More men in prime of life spend less time working, p. 1.

New York Times (October 15, 1995). Black men say the march in Washington is about them, not Farrakhan, p. 22.

New York Times (February 25, 1996). Corporations under fire (editorial).

New York Times (February 27, 1996). Downsizing statistics don't show the pain, p. 16.

New York Times (May 20, 1996). A temporary force to be reckoned with, p. D1.

New York Times (August 18, 1996). A new era of ups and downs: volatility of wages is growing, p. 1.

Ovesey, L. (1962). Fear of vocational success. *Archives of General Psychiatry*, 7:82–92.

Piers, G. and Singer, M. B. (1953). *Shame and Guilt: A Psychoanalytic and a Cultural Study*. Springfield, IL: Charles C Thomas, 1971.

Pine, F. (1990). *Drive, Ego, Object, and Self: A Synthesis for Clinical Work*. New York: Basic Books.

Plaut, E. A. (1979). Play and adaptation. *The Psychoanalytic Study of the Child*, 34:217–232. New Haven, CT: Yale University Press.

Pruyser, P. (1980). Work: Curse or blessing. *Bulletin of the Menninger Clinic*, 44:59–73.

Reich, A. (1960). Pathological forms of self-esteem regulation. *The Psychoanalytic Study of the Child*, 15:215–232. New York: International Universities Press.

Rosener, J. (1992). Ways women lead. In J. J. Gabarro (Ed.) *Managing People and Organizations*. Boston, MA: Harvard Business School Publications.

Ross, J. M. (1994). *What Men Want*. Cambridge, MA: Harvard University Press.

Satow, R. (1988). Psychic functions of failure. *Psychoanalytic Review*, 75:443–457.

Schor, J. B. (1992). *The Overworked American*. New York: Basic Books.

Shapiro, J. L., Diamond, M. J., and Greenberg, M. (1995). *Becoming a Father*. New York: Springer.

Socarides, C. W. and Kramer, S. (Eds.) (1997). *Work and Its Inhibitions: Psychoanalytic Essays*. Madison, CT: International Universities Press.

Stark, M. (1989). Work inhibition: A self-psychological perspective. *Contemporary Psychoanalysis*, 25:135–158.

Super, D. E. (1957). *The Psychology of Careers*. New York: Harper and Row.

Tannen, D. (1995). *Talking from 9 to 5: Women and Men in the Workplace*. New York: Avon Books.

Tartakoff, H. H. (1966). The normal personality in our culture and the Nobel Prize Complex. In R. M. Loewenstein, L. M. Newman, M. Schur, and A. J. Solnit (Eds.) *Psychoanalysis: A General Psychology*. New York: International Universities Press.

Vaillant, G. E. (1993). *The Wisdom of the Ego*. Cambridge, MA: Harvard University Press.

Wallerstein, R. S. (1986). *Forty-two Lives in Treatment: A Study of Psychoanalysis and Psychotherapy*. New York: Guilford.

White, R. W. (1959). Motivation reconsidered: The concept of competence. *Psychological Review*, 66:297–333.

White, R. W. (1963). Ego and reality in psychoanalytic theory: A proposal regarding independent ego energies. *Psychological Issues Monograph 11*.

Wilson, W. J. (1997). *When Work Disappears*. New York: Random House.

Winnicott, D. W. (1950). Aggression in relation to emotional development. In *Through Paediatrics to Psychoanalysis*. New York: Basic Books, 1975, pp. 204–218.

Winnicott, D. W. (1971). *Playing and Reality*. New York: Basic Books.

Index

E

efficacy, feeling of, 5–6. *See also* mastery
ego functions, work and, 6–9, 41–42, 56
ego ideal, 10–12, 22, 30, 57
ego identity, 8–9, 21–22
ego-supportive interventions, 82–85
Erikson, E. H., 8–9, 11, 15, 21–22, 25, 27, 31, 33, 58

F

failure, 12–13, 67–69, 72. *See also* success
family, work and, 27–28, 48, 130–133
Fast, I., 36, 56
Freud, A., 15, 16
Freud, S., xx, 2–3, 7, 13, 36, 42, 71
Furman, E., 15

G

gender dynamics, 30, 80–81, 126–130
gender equity, 125–126
"generative leadership," 31–32
Gilmore, D., 127
Gould, R. L., 20
grandiosity, 23, 49, 57, 58, 61–64
Greenberg, M., x
Greenson, R. R., 127
group *vs.* solo work, 42, 90
Gunsberg, L., x
Gurwitt, A. R., x

H

Halpern, R., 136
Hartmann, H., 5, 8
Hendrik, I., 5–6
Herr, T., 136
hierarchies, 14, 42, 121–123
Hirschhorn, L., x, 3, 8, 13, 39, 115n, 116–118, 122
Hochschild, A., xv, 121, 131, 132, 139
Holmes, D., 7

I

idealizations, 11–12, 24, 56, 57, 85, 92, 94
ideals, 19, 30, 33, 56, 79
identifications, 21, 22, 24, 30, 80–81
identity, 8–9, 21–22, 55, 57, 113. *See also* work role

impossible projects. *See* work disturbance, diffusion
inhibition. *See under* work disturbance
integrity, sense of, 27, 33
interpersonal conflict, 56, 63, 72–75, 90, 92–93

J

Jahoda, M., 6
Jaques, E., 7, 12–13, 28–29

K

Kanter, R. M., 116, 119n, 119–121, 123
Kernberg, O. F., 1
Kets de Vries, M., xx, 36n, 43, 48–49, 68, 73, 115n
Klein, E., 20, 22, 25, 28–30
Kleinian perspective, 12–13. *See also* depressive position
Kohut, H., 11–12, 33, 83, 120
Kramer, S., xix, 15–16, 36, 43, 77, 119

L

Lantos, B., 1, 4–5, 9, 15–16
Laplanche, J., 10
Lasch, C., 120
latency phase, 11
leadership, 31–33, 118, 130
learning
  child's, linked to adult's working, 15–16, 57–58
  the treatment process and, 84
Lemann, N., xvii
Levinson, D., 20, 22, 25, 28–30
Levinson, M., 20, 22, 25, 28–30
love relationships, 1, 23–25, 117, 133. *See also* family

M

management theorists, 116
  Drucker, xvii, 3, 16, 116, 118, 125, 126, 129–130, 132, 134–135
  Hirschhorn, xx, 3, 8, 13, 39, 115n, 116–118, 122
  Kanter, 116, 119n, 119–121, 123
manhood, in changing workplace, 127–129, 132–133